ANCIENT
ENVIRONMENTS

THE PRENTICE-HALL FOUNDATIONS OF EARTH SCIENCE SERIES

A. Lee McAlester, Editor

STRUCTURE OF THE EARTH

S. P. Clark, Jr.

EARTH MATERIALS

W. G. Ernst

THE SURFACE OF THE EARTH

A. L. Bloom

EARTH RESOURCES, 3rd ed.

B. J. Skinner

GEOLOGIC TIME, 2nd ed.

D. L. Eicher

ANCIENT ENVIRONMENTS, 3rd ed.

C. R. Newton and L. F. Laporte

THE HISTORY OF THE EARTH'S CRUST

D. L. Eicher, A. L. McAlester, and M. L. Rottman

THE HISTORY OF LIFE, 2nd ed.

A. L. McAlester

OCEANS, 2nd ed.

K. K. Turekian

MAN AND THE OCEAN

B. J. Skinner and K. K. Turekian

ATMOSPHERES

R. M. Goody and J. C. G. Walker

WEATHER, 2nd ed.

L. J. Battan

THE SOLAR SYSTEM

J. A. Wood

3rd Edition

ANCIENT ENVIRONMENTS

Cathryn R. Newton

Syracuse University

Léo F. Laporte

University of California, Santa Cruz

 Prentice Hall, Englewood Cliffs, New Jersey 07632

Library of Congress Cataloging-in-Publication Data

NEWTON, CATHRYN R. (date)
   Ancient Environments / Cathryn R. Newton, Léo F. Laporte.—3rd
ed.
     p. cm.—(Prentice-Hall foundations of earth science series)
   Rev. ed. of: Ancient environments / Léo F. Laporte. 2nd ed. c1979.
   Bibiography: p.
   Includes index.
   ISBN 0-13-036476-2
   1. Paleoecology. I. Laporte, Léo F. II. Laporte, Léo F.
Ancient environments. III. Title. IV. Series.
QE720.N49 1989
560'.45—dc19   88-7880
                                   CIP

Editorial/production supervision: *Kathleen M. Lafferty*

Manufacturing buyer: *Paula Massenaro*

© 1989, 1979, 1968 by Prentice-Hall, Inc.

A Division of Simon & Schuster

Englewood Cliffs, New Jersey 07632

Printed in the United States of America

10 9 8 7 6 5 4 3 2 1

ISBN   0-13-036476-2

Prentice-Hall International (UK) Limited, *London*
Prentice-Hall of Australia Pty. Limited, *Sydney*
Prentice-Hall Canada Inc., *Toronto*
Prentice-Hall Hispanoamericana, S.A., *Mexico*
Prentice-Hall of India Private Limited, *New Delhi*
Prentice Hall of Japan, Inc., *Tokyo*
Simon & Schuster Asia Pte. Ltd., *Singapore*
Editora Prentice-Hall do Brasil, Ltda., *Rio de Janeiro*

FOR HANK AND GOSIA

CONTENTS

3

DEPOSITIONAL SYSTEMS AND ENVIRONMENTS   36

4

ORGANISMS AND ENVIRONMENTS   57

5

TAPHONOMY   81

6

PALEOENVIRONMENTAL AND PALEOECOLOGICAL ANALYSIS   97

7

ENVIRONMENTAL SYNTHESIS   112

8

ENVIRONMENTS IN CRISIS   139

PREFACE

This third edition represents an updating of *Ancient Environments* and an expansion of the book, to cover two exciting areas in sedimentary geology—depositional systems analysis and the study of mass extinctions. We thank the following individuals for reviews and discussions of the manuscript: David J. Bottjer, University of Southern California; Richard H. Lindemann, Skidmore College; Michael L. McKinney, The University of Tennessee, Knoxville; and Robert M. Schoch, Boston University. Thanks are also extended to Willis Newman, Lauret Savoy, Joel Thompson, Jason Wang, Michael Whalen, and George Dix for suggestions in planning the revised edition, and to Sharon Bortel for help with permissions.

Cathryn R. Newton
Léo F. Laporte

ANCIENT
ENVIRONMENTS

1

GEOLOGIC ENVIRONMENTS

The history of organisms runs parallel with, is environmentally contained in, and continuously interacts with the physical history of the earth. (George Gaylord Simpson. 1963. "Historical Science." In The Fabric of Geology, edited by C. W. Albritton, Jr. Reading, Mass.: Addison-Wesley, 26).

In our dynamic biosphere, rapid environmental changes are obvious. Every year countless news stories document property damage or loss of homes resulting from coastal erosion and the retreat of shorelines during winter storms. New oceanic inlets now occupy the sites of former housing tracts, while in other areas the accumulation of sand is forming new spits or islands. Accounts of many other environmental changes are available for the relatively recent past, such as the transformation of the Great Plains of North America into a "dust bowl" during the 1920s and 1930s, a consequence of an unusually prolonged drought and overcultivation; prior to and following these years the region was highly fertile. Further back in history, the famous snowy scenes in the paintings of sixteenth-century Flemish painter Pieter Brueghel record an anomalously cold interval—the "Little Ice Age" of A.D. 1500 to 1800. During this period European writers and painters provided fascinating documentation of a global cooling that lowered average European temperatures by an estimated 1.3°C. Humans and other organisms inhabiting these changing environments were compelled to adjust their lives accordingly.

Going still further back in time, we can see on the European and North American continents the record of the massive gravels, sands, and silts left by repeated incursions of huge ice sheets during the Pleistocene epoch, spanning the last 2 million years. Not only did the ice destroy many habitats of land animals and plants, but the accompanying climatic cooling drove other organisms on land and in the sea into more temperate regions. Many organisms succumbed to the drastic upheaval in environment, resulting in Pleistocene extinctions.

But these contemporary and relatively recent changes in environment—whether induced by humans or natural processes—are not unusual events in Earth history. On the contrary, a study of Earth over its several-billion-year existence reveals continual changes in physical environments that in turn brought about changes in the organisms inhabiting those environments. Sometimes the environmental changes were even induced by the organisms themselves as, for example, when the rise of photosynthesizing organisms transformed the reducing atmosphere of early Earth to one rich in free oxygen.

The fossil record preserved in sedimentary rocks provides a very long history of important environmental fluctuations driven by both physical and biological mechanisms. This record is especially clear for the last half-billion years or so, owing to the abundant and increasingly diverse assemblage of organisms having fossilizable, mineralized skeletons. We discuss in this book the basic concepts and principles for interpreting such ancient environments through this interval of geologic time so well documented by fossils.

ENVIRONMENTAL STRATIGRAPHY
AND PALEOECOLOGY

This volume explores two approaches to understanding ancient environments and the organisms that inhabited them. The first, *environmental stratigraphy*, seeks to reconstruct the dynamics of ancient sedimentary environments using techniques from sedimentology along with knowledge of the life habits of the fossil fauna and flora. The ultimate goal of environmental stratigraphy is to define the physical, chemical, and biological aspects of the original depositional habitat. Of course, because many of the crucial environmental variables—such as temperature, salinity, and current velocity—are not directly observable in sedimentary rocks, other factors must be used in environmental reconstruction. The most important of these observable factors are grain size and composition, primary structures, geochemistry, and fossils. Our knowledge of these factors in various modern environments enables us to recognize the ancient counterparts of these habitats.

Another approach to the analysis of ancient environments is *paleoecology*, which is the study of the relationships of fossil organisms among themselves and with their local physical environments. Thus, the goal of paleoecology is to define the living habits of fossil organisms, the interactions of groups of organisms, and the relationships between sediments and animals or plants. Paleoecology therefore differs from environmental stratigraphy in its ultimate objectives, being more concerned with the interactions of fossil organisms than strictly with environmental recognition and classification.

Paleoecology is also related to the field of *ecology*, which deals with the interactions among living animals and plants and between these organisms and their habitats. We recognize two major subfields within the science of ecology, each of which has a counterpart within paleoecology. *Synecology* examines the dynamics of groups of species as they relate to each other and to the environment. *Autecology*, in contrast, seeks to understand the living habits of a single species, including such aspects as feeding, locomotion, and relationship with the physical environment. For example, the synecology of a Pacific coral reef involves the population size and structure of reef-building species and the parrot fishes that prey upon them, the effects of intense daily surf and periodic storms on the reef and reef-associated species, and the roles of sunlight and nutrients in controlling the growth of reef-building corals and their predators. In contrast, the autecology of a particular species living within the reef, say a sea urchin, would seek to explain where, specifically, the animal lives, how it feeds, how it avoids predators, and how it responds to water turbulence and changing levels of sunlight, salinity, and temperature. A similar distinction can also be made between *paleosynecology*, the analysis of groups of fossil species, and *paleoautecology*, the study of single species in the fossil record.

Some of the general principles of ecology can be applied to reconstruction of ancient ecosystems. A paleosynecological analysis of a Silurian coral reef might examine the particular marine conditions that favored the proliferation of rugose and tabulate corals, delicate crinoids, grazing snails, and robust trilobites and would investigate how these organisms interacted with each other spatially (Fig. 1-1).

But the long spans of geologic time represented by fossil assemblages and sedimentary strata mean that paleoecology cannot simply be construed as modern ecology projected backward in time. The durations of fossil communities or associations can often be measured in millions or tens of millions of years. Clearly, then, we cannot uncritically apply ecological principles based on experiments lasting a few months or years to the longer-duration patterns of fossil distribution and abundance observed in the rock record. Events occurring over short time spans— birth and death of individuals, social interactions within a population, even immigration to and emigration from a population—are very unlikely to be recorded in fossil assemblages.

It is necessary, therefore, to view ecological and paleoecological processes as operating over a *temporal hierarchy* (Fig. 1-2). *Individual organisms* experience birth and death, with ecological pressures in between; for most marine invertebrates these events occur on time scales of days to years. In contrast, the phenomenon of *ecological succession* operates on time scales of decades to centuries. For example, one may observe that following a California fire, grasses are the initial colonists of a landscape. Within several years, small trees form a low forest and shrub topography, and eventually these are succeeded by a large canopy of redwoods. Such a process may require hundreds of years to be completed (the so-called climax community). Of course, ecological succession may in many cases never attain the final

A

B

FIG. 1-1 These reconstructions of a Silurian reef community show the inferred life habits of middle Paleozoic colonial rugose and tabulate corals, crinoids (sea-lillies), predaceous nautiloid cephalopods, and grazing snails in this patch-reef environment. Such a reconstruction represents pictorially what the science of paleoecology seeks in part to describe and explain. (A) Overview of the patch-reef environment. (B) Close-up of nautiloid cephalopod, corals, and snails. (Photos courtesy of Milwaukee Public Museum.)

	Phenomenon	Time Scale (years)
PALEOECOLOGY	Community Evolution	100,000 - 10,000,000 yrs
	Community Replacement	100 - 1,000,000 yrs
ECOLOGY	Ecological Succession	1 - 1000 yrs
	Community Establishment	0.001 - 1 yr

FIG. 1-2 Temporal hierarchy of ecological versus paleoecological processes. (After W. Miller, 1986).

stage, being interrupted too frequently by environmental disturbances (for example, if fires recur often).

On a far larger time scale are changes observed in fossil "communities." *Community replacement,* the environmentally influenced substitution of one fossil assemblage by another, may proceed at time scales of hundreds to millions of years. True *community evolution* in the fossil record refers to major evolutionary changes in associated groups of organisms. These changes, although not wholly independent of environmental influences, are primarily controlled by species-to-species interactions over evolutionary time—hundreds to millions of years, or even longer in some cases. A controversial example of community evolution has been proposed by Robert Bakker, at the University of Colorado, who claims that rapid evolutionary radiation of flowering plants during the Cretaceous period was triggered by predation by dinosaurs. In his view, heavy and extensive grazing by dinosaurs transformed terrestrial plant communities from conifer-dominated to angiosperm-dominated systems.

Thus, although some ecological principles can aid in interpreting the fossil record, for the most part we are dealing with very longterm patterns, some of which are environmentally mediated (community replacement) and some of which are evolutionarily controlled (community evolution).

PALEOECOLOGY, ENVIRONMENTAL STRATIGRAPHY, AND THE EARTH SCIENCES

Although it is intrinsically interesting to understand the ecology and environmental context of ancient organisms, paleoecology and environmental stratigraphy also have useful applications to related fields of geologic inquiry.

Paleoecology contributes most directly to *paleontology,* which is concerned with the history and evolution of life. Paleontologists, in analyzing the fossil record, seek more than merely a description of the various animals and plants that lived in the past; often they also wish to know how the size and shape of a fossil organism may have related to its ecology. To understand the dynamics of organic evolution, it is critical for paleontologists to place fossil organisms in their ecological and environmental contexts.

Environmental stratigraphy not only provides information regarding the distribution of ancient lands and seas but also documents more precisely the nature of these environments. Thus, environmental stratigraphy contributes directly to *paleogeography,* the study of the spatial configurations of ancient environments (including continent-ocean relationships). An excellent example of the use of environmental stratigraphy in paleogeographic reconstruction is shown in Fig. 1-3, which portrays sedimentary characteristics and inferred environments in Carboniferous rocks of Pennsylvania. Because many such environments are sensitive to climatic or

FIG. 1-3 Detailed analysis of the Pocono Formation, Carboniferous period, of the central Appalachians. This study by B. R. Pelletier examined many aspects of this sedimentary rock unit, including grain size and composition, orientation of cross-stratification and plant remains, maximum size of quartz pebbles, sand/shale ratios, and fossil content. Pelletier was able to demonstrate that the Pocono Formation was a nonmarine, coastal plain sediment derived from sedimentary rocks and low-grade metamorphic rocks in a source area located near Atlantic City, New Jersey. Sediment transport was to the west and northwest; the ancient shoreline trended northeast across Pennsylvania and was located some 25 miles east of Pittsburgh. Offshore the Pocono Formation is a marine shale and sandstone that contains abundant burrows ("*Arthrophycus*"), occasional brachiopods, and a few clams and snails. Sand/shale ratio greater than 2 is shaded; maximum pebble diameters in millimeters are shown by contours; current directions are shown by small arrows. Note relation of oil pools (black) to the sandbar belt. (After B. R. Pelletier, 1958.)

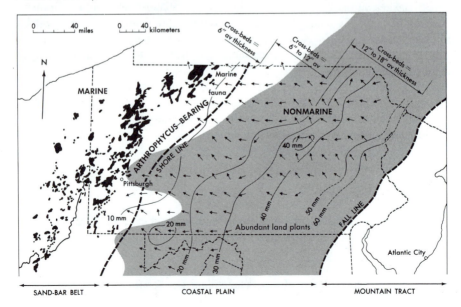

oceanographic variations, environmental stratigraphy can also contribute much information to studies of *paleoclimatology* and *paleoceanography*.

Finally, environmental stratigraphy and paleoecology can also be applied to the exploration for oil and gas deposits. These fossil fuels accumulate from the decomposed remains of microscopic marine organisms in sedimentary rocks. The porous and permeable sedimentary rocks that form hydrocarbon reservoirs are produced more readily in some environments than others—for example, coral reefs and sandbar deposits commonly make excellent reservoirs. For this reason, environmental stratigraphy can be an extremely powerful predictor in hydrocarbon exploration.

ENVIRONMENTAL CLASSIFICATION

Prerequisite to the reconstruction of ancient environments and the paleoecology of the fossils that inhabited them is a broad knowledge of the range of modern habitats, yet we must recognize that those environments in which sediment deposition is most rapid will be more frequently represented in the fossil record. For this reason many environments of intense interest to ecologists—tropical rain forests, for instance—are not emphasized by modern sedimentologists, because such a habitat (in which erosion predominates, or in which sedimentation is extremely low) is unlikely to preserve a record that can be analyzed paleoecologically or paleoenvironmentally. The stratigraphic record is thus biased to a certain extent, with high-sedimentation habitats being more completely represented. This in turn biases the fossil record because organisms are more likely to be preserved in areas of high sedimentation.

The environmental classification presented here is based on physical criteria, although by implication chemical factors (e.g., oxygen content) are also involved. Moreover, since virtually all environments are populated by different kinds of species, by extension these environments must also presuppose certain biological factors, and often the boundaries between these habitats are gradational. Nonetheless, these environmental categories are all readily recognizable in modern and also ancient contexts.

For each major sedimentary environment it is useful to identify the *medium* of deposition (marine, freshwater, or subaerial), the *process* that generates the physical energy that in turn affects the organisms and moves or deposits sediments (waves, tides, rivers, wind, and so on), and the *site* of deposition (beach, deep-sea floor, tidal flat, lake bottom, desert, and so on). Try to keep these categories in mind during our discussion of particular sedimentary environments.

Marine Environments

Environments within the world's oceans can be broadly subdivided into two major realms: the *pelagic,* which refers to the water mass itself, and the *benthic,* which refers to the seafloor beneath. The pelagic realm in turn can be subdivided into the water that overlies the continental shelves (*neritic*) and the water mass that lies beyond the continental shelves within the deeper ocean basins (*oceanic*). Areas within the pelagic and oceanic environments that receive enough sunlight to sustain the plant photosynthesis are within the *photic zone,* which is usually at depths above 200 meters; beneath this, the amount of light rapidly decreases, so that most of the ocean is within the *aphotic zone* (Fig. 1-4).

The benthic realm also has subdivisions that correlate approximately with the pelagic subdivisions. Thus, the *subtidal* environment includes the benthic areas of the continental shelves and hence is overlain by the neritic pelagic environment. The seafloor beyond the continental shelves includes the *bathyal, abyssal,* and *hadal* regions, corresponding roughly to the continental slope, the deep-ocean floor, and the deep-sea trenches, respectively.

The part of the seafloor that lies within the range of high and low tides is referred to as the *intertidal* environment. The narrow fringe of land that lies above the normal high-water mark but is still within range of marine influence (salt spray,

FIG. 1-4 Major marine environments as commonly defined. Although boundaries are not precise, note the general correspondence of subtidal, bathyal, abyssal, and hadal environments with continental shelf, slope, abyssal plain, and trench. The penetration of sunlight decreases with water depth, being virtually absent in waters deeper than about 200 meters, where it is always dark. The absolute depth of the photic zone depends, in part, on the density of organisms and suspended sediment in overlying waters. Because it is not always possible to distinguish supratidal, intertidal, and shallow subtidal environments in sedimentary rocks, the more general, inclusive term *peritidal* is commonly used.

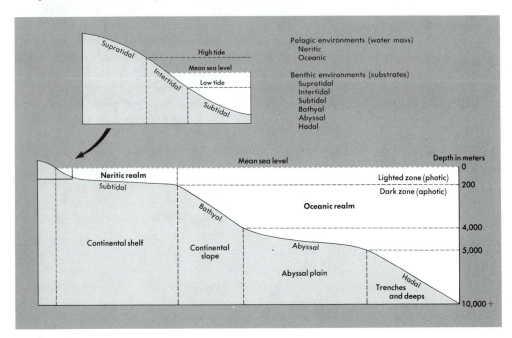

storm waves, or unusually high tides) is defined as the *supratidal* environment. Because we cannot usually distinguish these two environments, the term *peritidal* is often used to include both. These various marine environments are illustrated in Fig. 1-4.

Terrestrial Environments

Terrestrial habitats are far more heterogeneous and variable than marine habitats. An excellent example of this greater variability can be seen in the global temperature ranges of terrestrial versus marine habitats (Fig. 1-5): Organisms inhabit a range some *three times greater* on land than in the ocean (more than 150°C compared with less than 50°C).

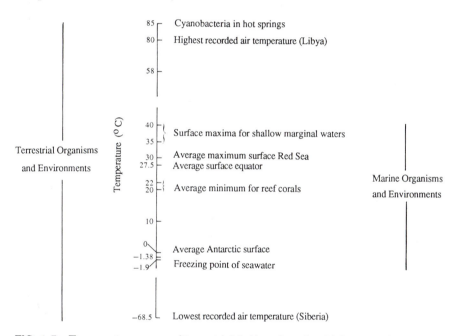

FIG. 1-5 Temperature range of terrestrial (left) and marine (right) organisms of the biosphere, based upon recent historical records. (From J. W. Valentine, 1973.)

Nonmarine aquatic environments. Many varieties of aquatic habitats occur within the terrestrial realm, including *lacustrine* (lakes and ponds), *fluvial* (streams and rivers), and *swamp* environments. Important environmental factors in these aquatic environments are the intensity of currents and the ratio of water-surface area to water depth. Current energy controls the rate of supply of nutrients and food and, in the case of strong currents, may also affect the movement of organisms. The ratio of water-surface area to depth influences the amount of vertical mixing and aeration that can take place. In shallow streams and ponds there is usually enough oxygen in the water column to support a rich flora and fauna. By contrast, deep lakes often have only a shallow aerated zone and are oxygen-depleted at depth, so that only infrequently will oxygen-using organisms be able to inhabit deep lake-floor environments.

Nonaquatic terrestrial environments. In nonaquatic terrestrial habitats, physical conditions such as temperature, humidity, wind, and sunlight may fluctuate considerably daily or seasonally. Besides temporal variations in physical conditions, there is also marked geographic variation because of topography, latitude, or oceanic climate. The result is a series of widely different dry-land habitats, including deserts, semiarid plateaus, arctic tundra, and rain forests. Taken as a whole, these environments are much more variable than the marine environment or aqueous nonmarine environment. We noted earlier that many of these terrestrial habitats (rain forests, for example) are not sites of active sediment deposition and hence do not usually occur in the stratigraphic record. Table 1-1 indicates major depositional environments for which there are frequently ancient counterparts. Figure 1-6 also illustrates the lateral relationship between terrestrial and nearby marine environments.

Table 1-1 Major Environments of Deposition

TERRESTRIAL	MARINE
Subaerial	Nearshore (subaerial to subaqueous)
Landslide and talus	Marshes
Dunes and desert pavement	Dunes
Lacustrine	Tidal flats
Lakes and ponds	Beaches
Swamps	Deltas
Fluvial	Lagoons
Alluvial fans	Estuaries
Rivers and Streams	Bays
Flood plains	Offshore
Deltas	Shallow subtidal (inner continental shelf)
	Deep subtidal (outer continental shelf)
	Continental slope
	Deep sea
	Organic buildups
	Wave-built (e.g., shell mounds)
	Organism-built (e.g., coral reefs)

ENVIRONMENTS THROUGH TIME

Paleoecology and environmental stratigraphy are powerful approaches for interpreting organism-environment interactions at selected times in Earth history (as, for example, the analysis of the Silurian reef in Fig. 1-1). But they are perhaps even

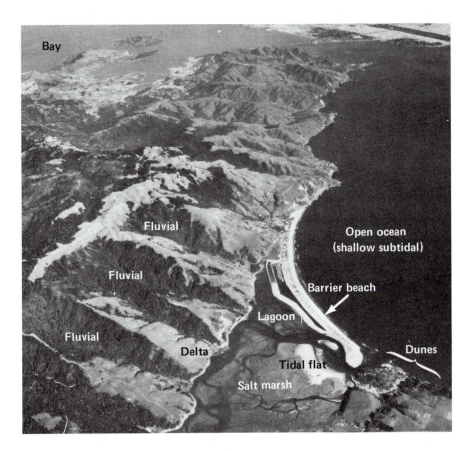

FIG. 1-6 Oblique aerial view of coast just north of San Francisco, California, showing the variety of environments from fully terrestrial to fully marine. Several of the major environments of deposition listed in Table 1-1 are identified.

more interesting when used to document major changes in organism-environment relationships during geologic time. Using paleoecology and environmental stratigraphy, we can see three major types of environmental change in Earth history: *frequently repeating, infrequently repeating, and irreversible.* When repetitions occur with fairly strict regularity, they are referred to as *cycles.*

Frequently repeating changes are environmental oscillations that have relatively short geologic duration. An example is the fluctuation of the thickness and areal extent of the Pleistocene ice sheets in North America. Expansion of ice during glacial intervals was also associated with global cooling and lowering of sea level, so that both terrestrial and marine systems were strongly affected. The fossil record of this geologic time interval reveals high-frequency environmental changes with cycles of 23,000, 41,000, and 100,000 years—rates of change that are very rapid in geologic terms. Many paleoclimatologists now believe that these ice-age cycles were triggered by changes in Earth's orbital geometry with respect to the sun, such as variations in the axis of rotation and in the shape of the elliptical orbit of Earth about the sun. The climatic effects of orbital oscillations were documented 70 years ago by the Yugoslav engineer Milutin Milankovitch but have only in the last few decades been widely accepted as important causes of the Pleistocene ice ages. These *Milankovitch cycles* are now known from the Pleistocene and also have been documented by environmental stratigraphers and paleoecologists from many portions of the Phanerozoic fossil record (see Chapter 7 for more about these cycles). While the cycles left a record of climatic change in many Phanerozoic sedimentary deposits, only when the continents were properly positioned did the cycles result in glaciation.

A second pattern of environmental and paleoecological change involves infrequent and episodically repeating variation. Recently, D. M. Raup and J. J. Sepkoski, at the University of Chicago, have claimed this sort of long-term episodicity in mass extinctions. Based on global compilations of marine diversity, they recognize a 26-million-year periodicity in Mesozoic and Cenozoic mass extinctions. In their view—not accepted by all paleontologists—most of the fossil record is dominated by normal levels of speciation and extinction, with much higher than average rates of extinction every 26 million years. The driving mechanism for this periodicity is even more controversial. Many workers interpret this infrequent, episodic pattern as evidence for an extraterrestrial cause of mass extinctions, asteroid impact being the most widely cited of these extraterrestrial mechanisms. However, other Earth-bound mechanisms, such as sea-level fluctuations, mountain-building, and long-term climatic change may also occur in infrequent and episodic patterns, so the debate continues.

A third kind of environmental change in geologic history includes the *non-repeating, irreversible* events that make the earth a significantly different world from time to time. Many of these events are triggered by the organisms themselves—for example, the origin of photosynthesizing organisms transformed the earth's atmosphere irreversibly from an environment rich in carbon monoxide and carbon dioxide (with lesser amounts of methane and ammonia) to one rich in nitrogen and oxygen. This transformation also had other consequences for the paleoecology of the planet, for with the change came the evolution of the ozone layer in the upper atmosphere, which shields the earth's surface from much harmful solar ultraviolet radiation. This is only one among several known examples of biologically induced, irreversible changes in geologic environments.

These three types of environmental change have important implications for paleoecology and environmental stratigraphy. Recognition of these profound environmental variations—frequent, infrequent, and irreversible—implies that our present-day biosphere cannot always serve as the only model for ancient biological assemblages. Evolutionary changes in the organisms, too, are in the broadest sense irreversible, so that comparisons of modern organisms with ancient ones may not always be warranted. In many cases, the present is a reasonable starting point for interpreting the past but one that ought to be used cautiously. The geological dictum that "the present is a key to the past" must therefore be applied judiciously.

Uniformitarianism refers to the use of modern geologic processes and relationships to reconstruct events and configurations in Earth history. We recognize two distinct kinds of uniformitarianism. *Methodological uniformitarianism,* which is useful in paleoenvironmental and paleoecological analysis, states that physical and chemical processes operating on the earth obeyed the same fundamental laws in the geologic past that they do today. For instance, we infer that the principles of thermodynamics applied equally as well 65 million years ago as they do today. In contrast, another form of uniformitarianism, *substantive uniformitarianism,* which holds that Earth processes and configurations of the past are essentially identical to those of today, is certainly not valid because of regularly repeating, irregularly repeating, and irreversible changes, including variations in sea level, extent of glaciation, and global biological diversity.

PLAN OF THE BOOK

The next three chapters deal with sediments and environments and with organisms and environments. The fifth chapter explores *taphonomy,* the study of the processes of fossilization, from the time of an organism's death until the fossil is discovered. The two chapters thereafter deal with paleoecological and paleoenvironmental analysis and their synthesis, with specific case studies presented in some detail. The final chapter emphasizes an important theme in current paleoecological research: the pattern and processes involved in mass extinctions.

This volume, which emphasizes the paleoecological and environmental reconstruction of past events, is complementary to other volumes in this series, particularly *The History of Life,* by A. Lee McAlester; *Geologic Time,* by Don L. Eicher; and *The History of the Earth's Crust,* by Don L. Eicher, A. Lee McAlester, and Marcia L. Rottman.

SUMMARY

Paleoecology is the study of the dynamic relationships among groups of fossil organisms and between those ancient organisms and their environments. It shares some overlap with the science of ecology, which studies the biological interactions and environmental context of modern organisms. However, paleoecology deals with biological interactions on time scales of thousands, millions, even tens of millions of years, whereas ecological observations are made on scales of months or years. For this reason, paleoecology is especially directed at answering many questions of long-range evolutionary significance.

Environmental stratigraphy is an allied field that uses both fossils and sedimentary attributes of rocks to interpret their original environment of deposition. Environmental stratigraphy and paleoecology can be viewed as important fields in their own right, but they can also be applied to problem-solving in the related fields of paleoclimatology, paleogeography, and paleoceanography.

The two disciplines of paleoecology and environmental stratigraphy contribute much to the reconstruction of individual ancient environments and also address broader questions of environmental change through geologic time. Because the earth's environments have varied episodically and irreversibly through time, we cannot uncritically apply modern biological and environmental models to the fossil record.

2

SEDIMENTS
AND ENVIRONMENTS

Behind the history of every sedimentary rock there lurks an ecosystem, but what one sees first is an environment of deposition. (Edward S. Deevey. 1965. Book review, Environments of the Geologic Past. Science 147:592.)

Sediments are deposits of solid material laid down on the surface of the earth by water, wind, or ice. These sedimentary deposits are as varied as beach sands, lake muds, stream gravels, coral rubble, and desert dunes. The two main sources of this variety are the origin of the sedimentary grains and the environment in which these grains are laid down. Another important variable in the study of sediments is what happens physically and chemically to them *after* deposition—through the processes of compaction, cementation, and recrystallization that turn the sediment into sedimentary rock. Therefore, we must consider three separate environmental influences responsible for the formation of sedimentary rocks, namely, (1) the genesis of the sedimentary grains in the source area, (2) the transportation of these grains and deposition in their final resting place, and (3) the transformation of the loose grains into a compact, lithified, sedimentary rock.

ORIGIN OF SEDIMENTARY GRAINS

We can distinguish two origins of sedimentary particles relative to the site where they are ultimately deposited. *Allochthonous** (from the Greek, meaning

---

*We will try to avoid technical jargon as much as possible, but in some instances the precision of technical language is necessary.

"from a different place") sediments result from the erosion and transportation of materials that originate at some distance from the place where they eventually accumulate. Thus, the Mississippi River annually deposits some 500,000 metric tons of sediment derived from a very large region that includes all or part of 31 states, or 41 percent of the total area of the contiguous United States. Rocky coastlines, too, are continually eroded by the surf along the sea's margins. The resulting erosional debris is deposited as local beaches and barrier bars, or it is carried along the coast by longshore currents and laid down a considerable distance from its place of origin.

In contrast, *autochthonous* (from the Greek, meaning "native to a place") sediments originate within the area of deposition. For example, shelly invertebrates such as clams, snails, and corals extract calcium carbonate from seawater to build their skeletons; when the organisms die, their shells are deposited with other accumulating sediments. In some hypersaline lakes and seas, salts such as sodium carbonate and calcium sulfate precipitate because of high rates of evaporation. There are various places in the world—such as Pakistan, the Soviet Union, and Germany, as well as New York, Kansas, and Michigan in the United States—where ancient salt deposits are profitably mined for table salt, gypsum, and potassium.

Sediments and rocks composed of grains that have been broken down and eroded as discrete particles from the source area are called *clastic* (from the Greek, meaning "broken"). Clastic deposits may represent a wide range of grain sizes (including boulders, pebbles, sand, or silt) and may reflect either local or long-distance transport. *Nonclastic* sediments and rocks form from skeletal materials of animals and plants or from chemical precipitates in seawater or lakes. Thus, the overall composition of a particular sediment or rock may reflect the characteristics of rocks in the eroded source area as well as the biological and chemical influences within the environment of deposition.

The composition of terrigenous clastic sediments also depends on the *rates* of both weathering in the source area and deposition in the sedimentary basin. If rocks in the source area are deeply weathered, then their constituent minerals are chemically altered and mechanically disintegrated. If erosional rates are rapid, then the minerals are transported and buried before much alteration and disintegration can occur.

Consider the weathering of granite, which is composed of quartz, mica, and feldspar. If the rates of weathering and transport are relatively slow, the micas and feldspars have ample time to break down into fine-grained clay minerals; the quartz grains may be rounded, but they are not altered chemically because of the great chemical stability of quartz. The resultant products of this granite therefore will be brought to the area of deposition as fine quartz sand mixed with finer-grained clays. The quartz sands may accumulate as nearshore or beach sands, while the clays are carried farther offshore in suspension, where they eventually settle out as mud. If this same granite had been subjected to more rapid rates of weathering and transportation, then the sedimentary deposits would have been quite different. The feldspars and micas would have been incompletely weathered and thus little altered and would be deposited as fine sand mixed with the quartz grains, yielding a sediment of different composition and texture (called "arkose") from that in the first case.

Rates of weathering, erosion, and transportation all depend strongly on climate and topographic relief in the source area. For example, wet climates favor chemical alteration of source rocks, because water plays an important role in many chemical weathering reactions. Rocks on steep slopes move more readily under the influence of gravity than rocks on more gentle slopes. Not only are landslides and soil creep aided by steep slopes, but the velocity of flowing water is greater, thereby allowing it to move more (and larger) erosional debris. Refer to Table 2-1, which illustrates major kinds of sediments and sedimentary rocks according to origin of sedimentary grains, their textures, and how they are deposited. We will now discuss some of these other aspects of sediments and sedimentary rocks.

Table 2-1 Origin and Classification of Major Sedimentary Rock Types

Weathering Processes	Weathering Products	Sediments	Rocks	
Physical disintegration	Pebbles of broken-up rock	Gravels	Conglomerates	Clastic Sedimentary Rocks
	Sand grains of resistant minerals, mainly quartz	Sands	Sandstones	
Physical and chemical breakup of easily altered minerals	New minerals, mostly clay-minerals	Muds	Shales	Nonclastic Sedimentary Rocks
Solution	Carbonates, chlorides, and sulfates in solution → Precipitation		Evaporates, mainly rock salt and gypsum	
	Extraction from solution by animals and plants	Mineralized skeletons	Limestones and cherts	
Extraction from soil by plants	Plant tissues → Decay of plants	Peat	Coal	

Source Rocks

(From L. F. Laporte, 1975.)

TRANSPORTATION AND DEPOSITION OF SEDIMENTS

Water is the principal agent of sediment transport. When water falls as rain it is, at first, quickly absorbed by the soil. Soon, however, the upper layers of the soil become saturated, and the rainwater begins to run off across the ground's surface. This surface runoff forms small rivulets that join to form brooks, streams, and eventually rivers.

During its overland journey the flow of water transports sedimentary materials in three different ways. First, the water takes into *solution* various substances such as calcium, iron, and carbon dioxide. Second, fine-grained minerals and rock fragments are carried in *suspension* in the turbulent flow of the running water. Third, the water flow moves coarse-grained particles by *traction,* bouncing and rolling them along the stream- or riverbed. Suspended and tractive sediments are eventually deposited in the delta at the river's mouth. Most of the dissolved load, however, goes directly into the sea, where it may either precipitate later (for example, by organisms as calcium carbonate) or remain in solution virtually indefinitely (for example, sodium chloride).

Ice, too, may be a significant agent of sediment transportation. At various times in Earth history, thick masses of snow and ice covered large parts of the continents. As snow accumulated and compacted under its own weight, it turned to ice and began to flow as a very plastic solid, expanding outward from its place of initial accumulation. These thick glacial masses inched inexorably forward, skimming off soil and weathered rock layers. Some of this glacially eroded debris became embedded within the glacier only to be washed out, perhaps many miles from where it was first gathered up, when the glacier ice eventually melted. The hummocky topography in the northern latitudes of the Northern Hemisphere is the result of the deposition of sand and gravel by Pleistocene glaciers, which were widespread in these areas.

Wind is a much less dense and less viscous medium than either water or ice and therefore usually carries far less sedimentary material in suspension or traction and virtually none in solution (although water vapor in the atmosphere may contain some dissolved salts). In areas where there is a poor cover of vegetation and where the climate is arid, there may be significant sediment transport by the wind, resulting in the formation of sand dunes. Windblown sand may also be a very effective erosional agent by abrading rock outcrops and exposing desert pavements.

Within marine environments, transportation of sediments is accomplished mostly by moving seawater, although there may be occasional rafting of sediment out to sea by debris-laden icebergs. Movement of sedimentary grains within the oceans is basically the same as that in streams, but although rivers and streams have confined channels along which sedimentary particles are transported, currents within the sea are often less well defined. For example, off the southeastern United States, the Gulf Stream sweeps across the Blake Plateau, a particularly wide extension—more than 300 kilometers in some places—of the continental slope. Although the water depths over the Blake Plateau range from about 200 to more than 1,000 meters, the surface of the plateau is only thinly veneered by recent marine sediments; rocks of Tertiary age crop out at or near the seafloor. Marine geologists infer that the broad surface of the Blake Plateau is swept clean of any sedimentary material by the Gulf Stream, whose axis of flow shifts periodically back and forth across the plateau.

The Gulf Stream is a *boundary current,* driven by global winds. Such boundary currents form parts of enormous oceanic gyres in all the major ocean basins; analogues to the Gulf Stream can be found off the coasts of Japan (the Kuroshio Current) and East Africa (the Agulhas Current). In contrast to these large-scale circulation patterns are the more localized *longshore currents* and *tidal currents,* which are the major controls on sediment transport along many coastlines.

A more episodic, but still volumetrically important, mechanism of sediment transport is the *turbidity current.* Owing to the great topographic relief of the seafloors, intermittent movement of watery muds and sands by gravity flow occurs. Such turbid, sediment-laden currents, which are often triggered by earthquakes, can erode older, consolidated marine sediments. It is likely that the lower parts of submarine canyons that cut across the continental shelves and slopes are carved out by such turbidity flows as material moves from the continental margins down into the abyssal plains of the deep-ocean basins. At the mouth of these canyons, sediment transport by turbidity currents generates *submarine fans* or *aprons* resembling river deltas.

The agents of sediment transport vary in their frequencies and in their capacities to carry materials. Consequently, there are often relatively long intervals during which sediments are not transported any significant distance in their journey from their source area to their final accumulation site. For example, significant quantities of sediment may be transported only during the flood stage of a river. If so, between floods, only the dissolved fraction and the fine-grained, suspended fraction of a river's sediment load will move downstream (Fig. 2-1). Sediments eroded in high, mountainous areas are deposited as alluvial fans within the adjacent valley floor, where they can remain for long periods of time. But eventually, they, too, are eroded and retransported, gradually progressing toward the delta at their river's mouth. As for sediments that accumulate initially along the continental shelves, oc-

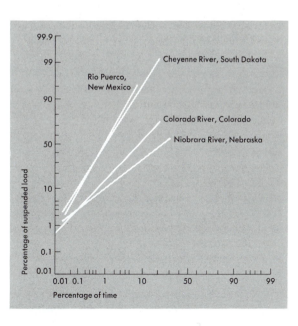

FIG. 2-1 Graphs of four rivers showing the times required to transport a given fraction of their suspended sediment load. Note that most of the suspended sediment is carried only a short part of the year, owing to annual variations in discharge of water in the rivers, which, in turn, reflect seasonal fluctuations in precipitation. Fifty percent of the suspended load is carried only about 4 days of the year for the Rio Puerco and Cheyenne, 31 days for the Colorado, and 95 days for the Niobrara. (After E. Wolman and J. Miller, 1960, Magnitude and frequency in geomorphic processes. *Journal of Geology,* v. 68, pp. 56, 59.)

casional turbidity currents will later transport some of this material still farther out to sea in the deeper parts of the oceans. Thus, although the net movement of sediment may be relatively slow by human standards, given the geologic time available for erosion, transportation, and deposition, the overall impact of these geologic processes is enormous.

Texture is a particularly useful characteristic in describing and interpreting a sedimentary rock. Texture refers not only to the size of the component grains but also to their shape and mutual arrangement within the enclosing matrix. Sedimentary textures provide clues to the nature of the depositing medium. For example, the size and angularity of stream-laid deposits increase exponentially with an increase in the velocity of stream flow and decrease with increasing distance from the source of the sediments. Sediments that are coarse grained, angular, and poorly sorted indicate rapid deposition close to the source area, often by swift-moving water. On the other hand, sediments that are fine grained, well sorted, and laminated suggest deposition far removed from the source area, in quiet water, where individual small grains settle slowly out of suspension. Experimental data, shown in Fig. 2-2, support this qualitative observation of the relationship between water velocity and size of material eroded, transported, and deposited. For sand-sized and coarser grains, increasingly larger grains are eroded and transported as water velocity increases.

FIG. 2-2 Graph showing size of grains that will be eroded, transported, or deposited at a given velocity. Notice that *cohesive,* fine-grained sediments resist erosion by high-velocity water in the same way that coarse sediments do. Also note that for grains of a given size, the velocity required for sedimentation, for transportation, and for erosion increases respectively. These experimental data reasonably approximate what is observed in nature. (From F. Press and R. Siever, 1974, *Earth,* San Francisco: W. H. Freeman and Co., p. 291.)

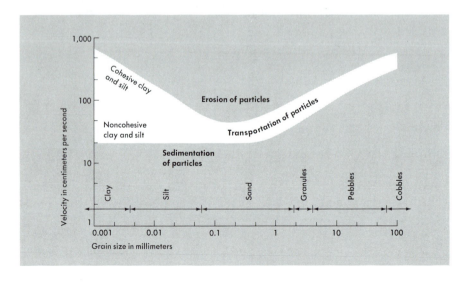

For particles smaller than sand—silt and clay—water velocities either decrease if the fine materials behave as discrete grains or increase if they cohere and behave as larger aggregates (as is frequently the case for clays). Note, too, that it takes more velocity to erode grains of a given size than to transport them, once eroded.

Transportation of sediments, especially by water, influences them in other ways besides determining grain size. The process of transportation causes individual grains to be rounded; finer-grained, clay-sized particles to be winnowed; and the grains to be better sorted. Consequently, sediment from a freshly weathered rock may start with angular, poorly sorted grains that include clay-sized particles but that become well-rounded and well-sorted, clay-free sand after considerable water transportation (Fig. 2-3).

FIG. 2-3 Processes of clay removal, grain-sorting, and grain-rounding. The role of each process varies with the amount of sediment transportation. (From J. M. Welles, 1960, *Stratigraphic Principles and Practices,* New York: Harper and Row, p. 341.)

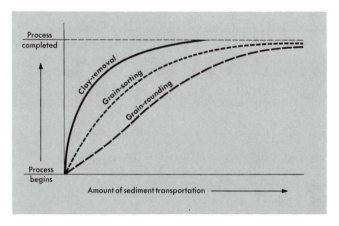

PRIMARY STRUCTURES

We have seen how the composition and size of sedimentary grains reflect differences among various depositional environments. We now consider how the arrangements of these grains within sediments and sedimentary rocks record some of the physical and biological attributes of the environments where they are deposited. These internal grain arrangements are called *primary structures* because they form during deposition or shortly after the sediments accumulate. Some primary structures, such as ripple marks or animal tracks and trails, form during sediment accumulation. Others, like mud cracks or animal burrows, develop soon after sediment deposition. In both cases, however, the primary structures are usually characteristic of the particular depositional environment and therefore often provide evidence about the nature of that environment. Of course, primary structures cannot be transported from one environment to another, so they are valuable environmental indicators. Some common primary structures of inorganic origin are described here, together with their environmental significance. In the section after this we will discuss how organisms by their activity not only generate primary structures but also contribute sediment themselves and thereby help build sedimentary rocks.

Cross-Stratification

An internal layering of sedimentary grains that is inclined to the principal surface of deposition is called *cross-bedding* or *cross-stratification* (see Fig. 2-4(A)). Cross-stratification may occur on a variety of scales; when individual cross-strata are thinner than 1 centimeter, the term *cross-lamination* is applied.

The inclination of cross-strata, which may be up to 30°, points in the direction of local current movement. Thus, it is possible to determine not only the general current direction but also the direction of the sediment's source (refer to Fig. 1-3). Because wind or water currents do not always flow in exactly the same direction, the geometry of cross-stratification within a sedimentary unit may vary considerably (see Fig. 2-4(A)). However, if a number of observations are made on cross-stratification, average regional directions of current flow can usually be determined.

Cross-stratification varies greatly, depending on the strength and regularity of current flow as well as the size and volume of sediments being transported. Detailed analysis of cross-stratification is thus an important part of defining and recognizing ancient sedimentary environments.

Ripple Marks

A surface of loose sediments may develop an undulating or rippled appearance as air or water currents move across it (Fig. 2-4(B)). Where the current is moving uniformly from one direction to another, the ripple marks will be asymmetrical, with their steeper sides facing downstream (or downwind), while oscillating currents will form symmetrical ripples. Like cross-stratification, asymmetrical ripple marks can be used to infer former current directions. In fact, cross-stratification is simply the cross-sectional representation of the surface rippling of a sedimentary bed. Both structures—one seen on the sediment surface, the other at right angles to it—are generated by the same physical process, namely, a moving current of water or air. As the force of the water or wind flow increases, sedimentary particles begin to move downcurrent or downwind. The surface of the sediment across which the water or wind flows becomes rippled owing to the movement of the particles (Fig. 2-5). If the flow is strong enough, however, all the surface particles move together, and the sediment surface appears smooth. Of course, the surface is also smooth or flat when there is no water or wind current, or if the current is not strong enough to move any sediment.

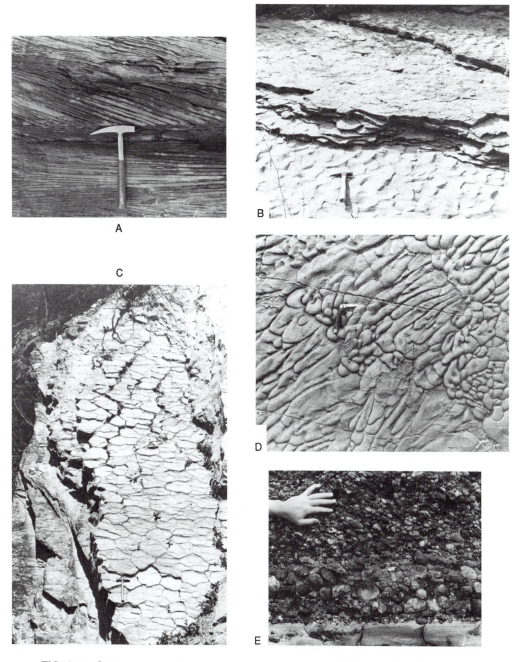

FIG. 2-4 Some common inorganic primary structures. (A) Three sets of cross-stratification in a Devonian sandstone where current moved from left to right. (B) Asymmetrical ripple marks in a Pennsylvanian sandstone where current moved from left to right. (C) Mud cracks in a Silurian limestone. (D) Sole markings on the bottom of an Ordovician turbidite bed where current flowed from lower left to upper right. (E) Graded bedding in a Paleocene conglomerate. (B, C, D from F. J. Pettijohn and Paul Potter, Springer-Verlag, New York, Inc.; A, E courtesy of Henry Mullins.)

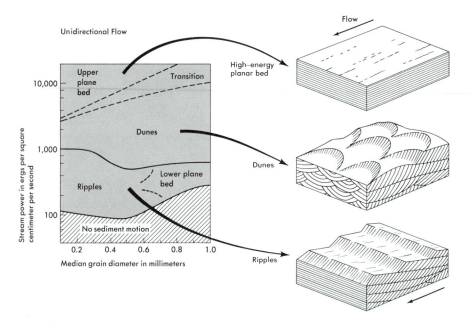

FIG. 2-5 Relationship between force of water flow and grain size in controlling the shape of the sediment surface. At low flow, there is no sediment motion; with increasing flow, the sediment surface becomes rippled and then dune-shaped; at high flow, all the sediment moves along the surface, leaving a plane, or flat, sediment surface. Not shown here are additional sedimentary structures that will form along the sediment surface at still higher flows. (After J. C. Ingle, Jr., 1975.)

Mud Cracks

Fine-grained, water-laid sediments that are later exposed to the air usually shrink and crack as they dry out. These desiccation cracks form irregularly shaped polygons whose size is proportional to the thickness of the layer being dehydrated and to the drying time (Fig. 2-4(C)). Although some muds form shrinkage cracks underwater (*syneresis cracks*), they do not have the typical connected polygonal pattern of air-dried, mud-cracked sediments. Mud cracks, therefore, provide evidence of periodic exposure to air and, if combined with other relevant evidence, may indicate periods of temporary or long-continued terrestrial conditions.

Sole Marks

Storm or turbidity currents have sufficient energy to erode the seafloor as the debris-laden current moves across it. The scour marks that are formed have a variety of characteristic forms, some of which indicate the direction from which the current came. The scour marks are usually preserved as casts formed by the coarse sediment that is deposited by the current after its eroding front has passed by. The casts of these scour marks thus appear on the sole, or bottom, of the sedimentary layer, hence the term *sole marks* (Fig. 2-4(D)). Other sole marks include local casts where the contact between sand and mud layers is deformed during compaction.

Graded Bedding

The sediment deposited by a waning current is usually laid down in such a way that the coarse grains are dropped first, followed by the settling out of the progressively finer grains. This change in texture occurs because as the current's velocity decreases, the coarsest pebbles and sand grains are deposited initially. (Refer to Fig. 2-2 to see why this is so.) This coarse layer is then slowly buried by finer-grained sand, silt, and clay as they, in turn, settle out of suspension from the overlying turbid water. This regular decrease in grain size from the base of a sedimentation unit to the top is called *graded bedding* (Fig. 2-4(E)). Although graded bedding can also be found in other sedimentary environments, it is typical of rock sequences laid by turbidity currents and, combined with other criteria, such as sole marks, can be useful in defining turbidity-current environments.

Figure 2-6 illustrates the vertical and lateral variation seen in a turbidite bed from its base to its top, from near its source (proximal) to some distance away from the source (distal). Graded bedding is best seen in unit A, which contains the coarsest sediment, usually medium to coarse sand. Unit B, composed of finer sand, shows parallel laminations and reflects deposition in a waning, but still strong, flow of water. (This is the "upper plane bed" of Fig. 2-6.) As the turbidity current further slackens with time and distance, unit C is deposited as a current-rippled, cross-stratified sand. (Refer again to Fig. 2-6.) Unit E records deposition of fine-grained sediments from suspension in the overlying water column following turbidite deposition. Unit D, then, is transitional from turbidite to pelagic deposition. Notice

FIG. 2-6 Vertical and lateral changes in grain size and primary structures in a turbidite bed. The actual thickness of the bed varies, on the average, from 10 centimeters to 1 meter near the source (proximal), and 1 to 10 centimeters some distance downcurrent (distal). The sediment grains in units A, B, and C are removed by the turbidity current itself along the depositional surface. The triangular plot in the upper right shows how the average grain size in each of these units reflects the declining power of the turbidity flow. The sediments in units D and E are pelagic; that is, they settle out of suspension from the overlying water column. See text for further discussion. (After J. R. L. Allen, 1970.)

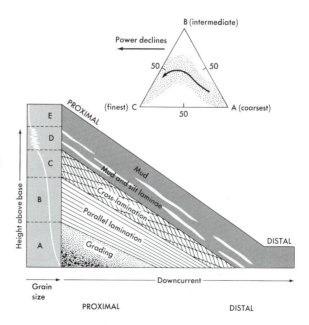

the correspondence between temporal and lateral changes in sediments as an important environmental parameter—water energy—varies. We will discuss other similar examples in which a vertical sequence of rocks records, over time, the same sort of environmental change one might see laterally at one moment in time.

ORGANIC INFLUENCES ON SEDIMENTS

Animals and plants can influence the composition and structure of sediments in several different ways. They contribute sedimentary grains by their skeletal debris. They also form organic primary structures by burrowing into and through sediments, destroying in the process preexisting inorganic structures like horizontal bedding or cross-stratification. Finally, organisms can build structures, like coral reefs or coastal marshes, that significantly modify local or regional patterns of sedimentation. Although we usually think of the physical environment controlling the behavior of organisms, it is equally true that plants and animals can modify the physical environment.

Organic Contribution to Sediments

Organisms contribute directly to sediments by producing a variety of internal and external skeletal materials such as bone, teeth, shells, or woody tissue, all of which become sedimentary grains after the death of the organisms. Within the marine sedimentary record, however, only the calcareous- and siliceous-secreting protistans (such as diatoms, radiolarians, and foraminifers) and the calcareous algae and invertebrates (including corals, brachiopods, bryozoans, molluscs, and echinoderms) have any quantitative significance in the sedimentary record. Limestones (variously estimated to make up 10 to 20 percent of sedimentary rocks) consist mainly of the calcareous skeletal grains of protists and marine invertebrates. Even today, large parts of the earth's seafloor are covered by a relatively thin veneer, up to tens of meters thick, of calcareous sands and silts derived over the last several million years from the skeletons of microscopic, floating single-celled organisms. In terrestrial environments, accumulation of plant remains is the first step in the formation of coal, a biological sediment that is the source of much of the world's energy.

Skeletal materials are weathered, transported, and deposited in much the same way as inorganically formed rocks and minerals. Most skeletal structures are secreted in an organic matrix that decomposes after the death of its owner. The organic matrix is attacked by microorganisms and is oxidized by oxygen in the atmosphere or in water. Consequently, the individual crystalline units that compose the skeleton and are embedded in this matrix are liberated and shed into the sediment. For example, a large clam shell that begins as a large, cobble-sized sedimentary grain will, as the binding matrix of the shell decomposes, eventually break down into many thousands of tiny calcite prisms and aragonite needles just a few micrometers long. Depending on the degree of decomposition, shelly sediments will thus have grain sizes and shapes that reflect the original internal architecture of the shell materials (Fig. 2-7).

After deposition, the organically produced crystalline remains, particularly some of the more unstable mineral types, such as aragonite and opal, are susceptible to solution, providing a reservoir of calcium carbonate and silica for later sediment cementation. The differing solubility of various kinds of skeletal debris can further bias any estimate about the original composition of the local flora and fauna based on fossil remains within a sedimentary rock. (The initial bias introduced, of course, is that of the nonpreservation of the many soft-bodied organisms that secrete no mineral material whatsoever.)

In short, then, through their secretion of various kinds of skeletal materials, organisms contribute directly and significantly to the ultimate composition and texture of a sediment. Because organisms in turn are limited in their distribution and abundance by the local environment (as will be discussed in the next chapter), the influence that the depositional environment exerts on the character of the accumulating sediments is demonstrated once again. Table 2-2 shows the distribution of skeletal minerals in the principal groups of animals and plants.

FIG. 2-7 A classic study of how a green calcareous alga (*Halimeda*) and a stony coral (*Acropora*) contribute skeletal debris to sediments. Note the wide variation in size from a few centimeters to several micrometers, depending on the degree of disarticulation and disintegration of the original skeleton. These two organisms thus can produce calcareous sediments of various textures from coral gravel to lime mud. (After R. Folk and R. Robles, 1964.)

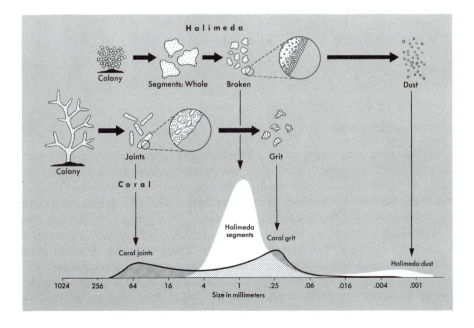

Table 2-2 Distribution of Skeletal Minerals in the Principal Phyla of Organisms

Kingdoms	Phyla		Calcium Carbonate CaCO₃		Opaline Silica SiO₂·nH₂O	Calcium Phosphate Ca₃(PO₄)₃OH
			Calcite	Aragonite		
Bacteria	Schizomycophyta					
	Cyanophyta (Cyanobacteria)		Frequent			
Protists	Chrysophyta	Diatoms			Common	
		Coccolithophorids	Common			
	Pyrrophyta					
	Sarcodina	Radiolarians			Common	
		Foraminiferans	Common			
Plants, fungi	Chlorophyta (Green algae)			Common		
	Charophyta (Stone worts)		Frequent			
	Phaeophyta (Brown algae)					
	Rhodophyta (Red algae)		Common			
	Mycophyta (Fungi) Bryophyta (Mosses) Tracheophyta (Vascular plants)					
Animals	Porifera (Sponges)		Frequent		Common	
	Coelenterata (Corals)			Common		
	Bryozoa (Bryozoans)*			Common		
	Brachiopoda (Brachiopods)		Frequent			Frequent
	Mollusca	Snails*	Frequent	Common		
		Clams*		Common		
		Cephalopods		Common		
	Annelida (Segmented worms)*		Frequent			
	Arthropoda	Trilobites Crustaceans	Frequent			Common
		Arachnids Insects				
	Echinodermata (Echinoderms)		Common			
	Chordata	Acorn worms Tunicates, lancelets				
		Vertebrates				Common

☐ Rare or absent

▨ Frequent

■ Common

*Mixed calcite–aragonite skeletons often occur in these groups.

(Modified from A. L. McAlester, 1977.)

Biogenic Structures

Organisms contribute to sediments in other, less direct ways. Many marine organisms, especially worms, arthropods, and molluscs, burrow into sediments for shelter and food (Fig. 2-8). By so doing they disrupt bedding, obliterate primary structures, and increase seawater circulation within the sediments. Organisms that feed on sediment for its included organic matter may aggregate the sediment to form pellets as it passes through the digestive tract. In environments where sediment is reworked by organisms faster than it accumulates—because of either slow sedimentation rates or large populations of organisms—the resulting sediments may be so extensively homogenized that they retain none of the original inorganic primary structures (Fig. 2-9).

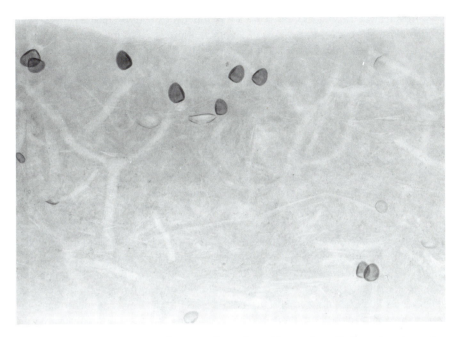

FIG. 2-8 X ray of marine sediments off southern Massachusetts in water several meters deep. Burrows were made by a variety of soft-bodied and shell-bearing invertebrates including crustaceans, polychaete worms, and bivalves. (Courtesy of D. C. Rhoads.)

FIG. 2-9 (A) Artificially laminated sediment with alternating layers of fine (dark) and coarse (light) sand in an aquarium. (B) Five marine worms were placed within the aquarium, and after 1 month the 4-1/2-inch bed of sediment was stirred up and the bedding obliterated. (Courtesy of R. N. Ginsburg, S.E.P.M. Special Publication No. 5.)

A   B

Besides modifying the character of sediments already deposited, organisms are also capable of altering patterns of sedimentation. For instance, thin mats composed of the intertwined filaments of various kinds of photosynthetic cyanobacteria and green algae can exert local, small-scale influence. These mats, which occur in shallow water (both fresh and marine) as well as on moist land surfaces, form tough, fibrous coverings on the sediment surface and thus inhibit or prevent the transport of grains along the surface. Hence, the mats act to keep sediments stable and free from erosion after their initial deposition.

Cyanobacterial mats are also capable of trapping and binding sediment grains on their gelatinous surface. As the mats are covered by newly deposited sediments, the bacterial filaments grow upward and form yet another mat. Successive periods of matting and deposition can result in a well-laminated sediment (Fig. 2-10). Furthermore, the geometry of these laminations is often related to the frequency and strength of local water movement.

Some of the oldest sedimentary rocks known contain laminated structures that are virtually identical with recent microbially laminated sediments. These rock structures, termed *stromatolites,* are believed to be microbial in origin, the layering or laminations being related to the successive development of mats, although the organic matter itself has not been preserved (Fig. 2-10). The presence of stromatolites in many Precambrian rocks, some of which are dated at 3 billion years or more, indicates the great antiquity of life—even if only "primitive" life. Stromatolites are also useful environmental indicators, because most rocks containing them were presumably deposited in shallow water, if we can assume that microbial mats occurred in the same environments in the past as they do today. In many cases this assumption appears justified, because stromatolites are produced by photosynthetic organisms and occur in close association with mud cracks and intraformational conglomerates, indicating subaerial exposure, desiccation, and local erosion of the accumulating sediments.

Geologically more dramatic examples of the organic modification of local patterns of sedimentation are provided by reefs. Organic reefs were most abundant in those parts of ancient seas that were clear, shallow, warm, well lit, and agitated, so that a profusion of shelly marine invertebrates flourished. Some of these organisms—such as stony corals, calcareous sponges, and certain massive bivalves—acted as *frame-builders* of these reefs. Other organisms—such as calcareous algae, bryozoans and hydrocoralline coelenterates—because of their encrusting mode of growth acted as the *cement,* binding the framework of the reef together into a rigid, wave-resistant structure. Other marine invertebrates—such as molluscs and echinoderms—provided the *detrital fill* for the growing reef mass (Fig. 2-11(A)).

Reefs can perpetuate the favorable conditions for their initial formation by growing as fast as the seafloor subsides, thereby maintaining the survival of the reef community in shallow water. With time the reefs become large masses of calcareous rock surrounded by nonreef sediments. In some cases the reefs form long, linear bodies that build up to sea level. This reef type has a quieter water lagoon behind the reef wall proper and a turbulent fore-reef environment. Thus, what began

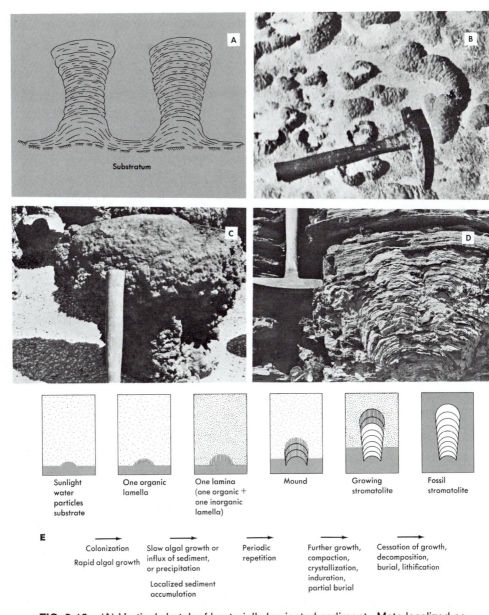

Sunlight
water
particles
substrate

One organic
lamella

One lamina
(one organic +
one inorganic
lamella)

Mound

Growing
stromatolite

Fossil
stromatolite

E

Colonization
Rapid algal growth

Slow algal growth or
influx of sediment,
or precipitation

Localized sediment
accumulation

Periodic
repetition

Further growth,
compaction,
crystallization,
induration,
partial burial

Cessation of growth,
decomposition,
burial, lithification

FIG. 2-10 (A) Vertical sketch of bacterially laminated sediment. Mats localized as small mounds that grow upward as successive layers of sediment are trapped by successive generations of mat formation. (B) A number of small cyanobacterial mounds on the floor of a saline lake in western Australia. During part of year the lake floor is covered with water, and the algal mats are rejuvenated; hammer gives scale. (Courtesy of Brian W. Logan.) (C) Large single mound from the intertidal zone of Shark Bay, Australia; coarse shell debris surrounds the mound. (Courtesy of Brian W. Logan.) (D) Cross section of a fossil bacterial mound (or stromatolite) from Precambrian rocks, about 1 billion years old, of Montana. (Courtesy of Richard Rezak, U.S. Geological Survey.) (E) Series of events, from left to right, in the development of stromatolite. (From H. Hofmann, 1969.)

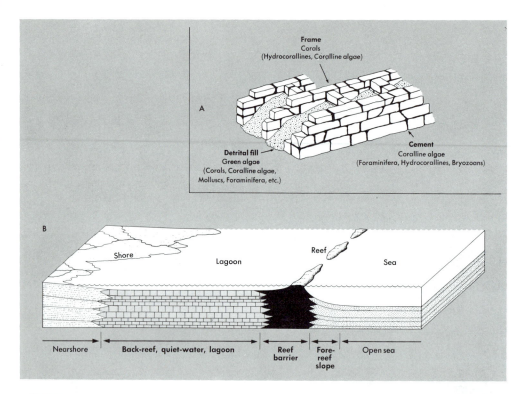

FIG. 2-11 (A) Schematic drawing of the role of various calcareous organisms in reef construction. Subordinate taxa in these three roles are listed in parentheses. (After R. N. Ginsburg and H. A. Lowenstam, 1958.) (B) Ancient reefs often had different kinds of organisms but they performed much the same structural function. As a reef develops, local patterns of sedimentation are altered; major subenvironments within a reef complex are the reef barrier and the environments in front of (more turbulent) and behind (less turbulent) the barrier. (C) Oblique aerial view of barrier reef, Belize, Central America. Deep water of the Caribbean to right; reef barrier, center; and shallow lagoon to left. (From R. K. Matthews, 1974.)

as an essentially uniform sedimentary marine environment is gradually transformed by reef development into several highly differentiated marine environments: *back-reef lagoon*, *reef barrier*, and *fore-reef slope* (Fig. 2-11(B,C)).

Significance of Organic Influence on Sediments

Having established that organisms contribute grains to sediments as well as disrupt their internal structures, we may reasonably ask how geologically significant such activity is. That is, given the rate at which these various biological processes occur, how great will the effects be in the geologic record?

Sedimentary rocks constitute about 75 percent areally and 5 percent volumetrically of rocks within the earth's crust. As we noted earlier, limestones—which are almost entirely biological in origin—probably account for 10 to 20 percent of the total. Hence, of the estimated 400 million cubic kilometers of sedimentary rock, 40 to 80 million are primarily the result of calcareous-secreting and -precipitating organisms. Although this is a startling figure in absolute terms, given the enormity of geologic time, slow depositional rates can easily account for such a great mass of biogenic calcareous sediments. For example, the present-day Bahama Islands in the Caribbean are underlain by shallow-water, shelly sediments that are at least 4,500 meters thick and that go back to the Early Cretaceous period. During the last 105 million years, therefore, some 4,500 meters of limestone have been deposited, giving an average accumulation rate of only 4.3 centimeters per 1,000 years. Such a rate surely must be minimal, however, because sedimentation has not been continuous owing to times of lowered sea level (as during the Pleistocene glaciations) when the Bahamas stood above water and were subjected to lithification and erosion.

Far higher accumulation rates of calcareous sediment are known for Bahamian shallow-water sediments during the last 5,000 years. Sediment accumulation rates for this interval in a lagoon on Little Bahama Bank range from 12 to 30 centimeters per 1,000 years. On still shorter time scales, organisms today are producing sediment even more rapidly than this: Growth rates for calcareous algae suggest that they produce up to three times as much sediment as accumulates within the lagoon, with the rest of the biological sediment transported in suspension over the bank margin and into deep-water environments. Thus, in some shallow carbonate environments, modern rates of biological sediment production greatly exceed long-term accumulation rates. This variation in sedimentation illustrates an important principle about the stratigraphic record, namely, that its formation is highly discontinuous and episodic. In general, therefore, the longer the duration of the interval in question, the slower the overall rate of sediment accumulation.

Estimates can also be made for accumulation rates of the minute calcareous shells of floating protistans that rain down on the floor of the deep ocean. For example, a core raised from deep-water sediments from an area south of the island of Hispaniola measures more that 900 centimeters, representing sediment accumulation during about 400,000 years. An average sedimentation rate for this Caribbean core is thus calculated at almost 2.5 centimeters per 1,000 years.

How do these shallow and deep-water rates of nonclastic carbonate sedimentation compare with areas of clastic sedimentation? In the Gulf Coast sedimentary basin, sedimentation rates are estimated at 20 centimeters per 1,000 years as averaged over the Cenozoic era. Once again, this is probably too low a figure because this area has, at times, been subject to repeated marine regressions and erosion and so has not continuously received sediments. Depositional rates for red clays in the deep-ocean basins are quite low, ranging from 1/20 to 1/2 centimeter per 1,000 years. Thus, sediments of organic origin are indeed being deposited at geologically significant rates that are comparable to, or greater than, those of many inorganic marine deposits.

In several instances marine biologists and geologists have measured the rate at which sediment is redeposited by various marine organisms. Often these rates are of the same order of magnitude as primary rates of inorganic and organic deposition. For example, many of the reef-dwelling fish of Bermuda (parrotfish, triggerfish, puffers, and the like) browse on the calcareous sand of the reef for its included food and for use as a milling agent in grinding the algae they have eaten. These fish annually redeposit between 2 and 3 metric tons of calcareous material per hectare (about 1 ton per acre) on a typical Bermuda reef. These data convert to a sedimentation rate of 10 to 15 centimeters per 1,000 years.

Burrowing marine invertebrates can also redistribute and redeposit materials after their initial deposition. Various studies—for example, of worms, holothurians (sea cucumbers), and clams—indicate that these organisms are capable of reworking sediment just as fast as or faster than it is deposited by inorganic agents. Some sediments may experience numerous episodes of burrowing prior to final deposition.

It seems clear, then, that organisms do make truly significant contributions to the sedimentary rock record through the formation of skeletal sedimentary grains as well as through the reworking and redeposition of sediment. In fact, when we once realize how effective organisms can be as rock-builders and sediment-modifiers, we may ask why *all* sedimentary rocks don't show these organic influences.

Some sedimentary rocks, such as evaporites, glacial deposits, and dune sandstones, will, of course, lack traces of any organic activity because they are formed in environments where organisms are virtually excluded. Other depositional environments may contain rock-building and sediment-modifying organisms, but the rate of organic activities is less than the rate of sediment influx and accumulation, so that the sediments are buried more rapidly than they can be effectively reworked by organisms. Hence, preservation of either inorganically produced primary structures (cross-stratification, ripple marks, graded bedding, and so on) or organically produced structures (burrows, pellets, shell beds) depends on the relative rates at which the inorganic and organic processes are working.

SUMMARY

Throughout this chapter we have stressed the importance of the local environment in controlling the genesis of a sedimentary rock. Thus, the composition of the source rock and the rate at which it is weathered influence the composition of the sedimentary grains brought to the basin of deposition. The nature of the transporting medium and the conditions existing during and after sediment deposition control the texture and primary structures of the sediments. The postdepositional environment determines the degree and kind of consolidation and lithification of the sediments into rocks. Organisms, too, contribute grains in the form of skeletal debris to the sediments, and the presence and distribution of organisms, in turn, is determined by the local environment. Organisms, moreover, can rework sediments to such an extent that original textures and structures are significantly altered.

3

DEPOSITIONAL SYSTEMS AND ENVIRONMENTS

Just as lateral facies changes give information on various environmental conditions in the same sedimentation area, observation of vertical facies changes is fundamental to study of changing environmental conditions in time. (Curt Teichert. 1958. Concept of facies. Am. Assn. Petrol. Geol. Bull. 42: 2739.)

At the moment of deposition, sedimentary units have areal dimensions that are closely related to the nature of the depositing medium. Stream and beach deposits are linear, running parallel to the direction of stream flow or surf action. Deep-sea muds and lagoon sands are blanketlike and usually widespread. Reefs and evaporite deposits are often quite discontinuous or patchy in their occurrence, and so their distribution is localized and irregular. With time, however, this two-dimensional geometry acquires a third dimension as a significant thickness of sediment accumulates. Thus, the three-dimensional character of an individual rock stratum may inform us about the particular depositional environment that formed it, whereas the vertical sequence of strata tells us what temporal changes occurred in the depositional environment. As we noted in Chapter 1, environmental stratigraphers and paleoecologists are as much interested in these changes in environments over time as they are in variations in environment over a geographic area at a specific moment. In this section, therefore, we will consider the environmental interpretation of depositional sequences seen in the stratigraphic record, in terms of both individual strata and their variation through time.

THE FACIES CONCEPT

Within a sedimentary basin there are usually a number of different local depositional environments. These local environments reflect variations in physical, chemical, and biological conditions as well as distance and direction from any depositional agent that may be entering the basin—such as a river with its associated delta. Hence, at any one time the sediments being deposited will have different characteristics that are correlated with the local depositional environments. Such lateral variations within a sedimentary basin are termed *sedimentary facies*. The depositional sites of these individual facies may also shift their position over time, so that each facies will have its own three-dimensional configuration in the overall stratigraphic sequence (Fig. 3-1).

Earlier we indicated that sediments have inorganic and organic attributes of texture, composition, internal structures, and fossils. Correspondingly, sedimentary facies may be characterized by their inorganic, lithologic qualities—*lithofacies*—as well as by their biological qualities—*biofacies*. Both lithofacies and biofacies are direct manifestations of the local depositional environment. In order to define and interpret the origin and history of a given stratigraphic section, it is useful to identify first the various sedimentary facies contained therein. Instead of speaking of "20 meters of Upper Cretaceous sandstone in this county and 50 meters of shale in the next" we may say "nearshore quartz sands here, passing into offshore shallow marine muds over there." The recognition and interpretation of facies thus permit us to move from a purely descriptive narrative of what is seen in scattered rock outcrops (a necessary first step) to a discussion of how and why certain kinds of rocks accumulated where they did, what were their spatial relationships, and what sorts of habitats might have existed for any related organisms.

Recognition and interpretation of lithofacies and biofacies are the crucial goals of environmental stratigraphy, which we discussed in Chapter 1. We will return to the facies concept again in Chapter 6, where we discuss in more detail the whole subject of environmental analysis. What we want to emphasize about the facies concept here, however, is that depositional environments at a given moment are not spatially uniform. On the contrary, they do vary markedly, and this variation is recorded by the different sediments and organisms found in each specific environment. As a result of this lateral variation in environment, we must always expect a particular sedimentary rock unit in the geologic record to change in facies, sooner or later, as we trace it laterally from one place to another. The facies concept is counter to an earlier, now-outdated, notion often referred to as the "layer-cake concept," whereby rock strata were visualized as relatively homogeneous layers that recorded uniform environments over large distances.

WALTHER'S LAW AND DEFINITION
OF STRATIGRAPHIC SEQUENCES

In 1894 the German geologist Johannes Walther noted that different kinds of sediments are deposited adjacent to each other as a result of lateral variations in depositional environments. He concluded that unless a significant gap occurs in the stratigraphic record, a vertical sequence of different sedimentary rocks must record the superimposition of those same environments over time. In other words, the se-

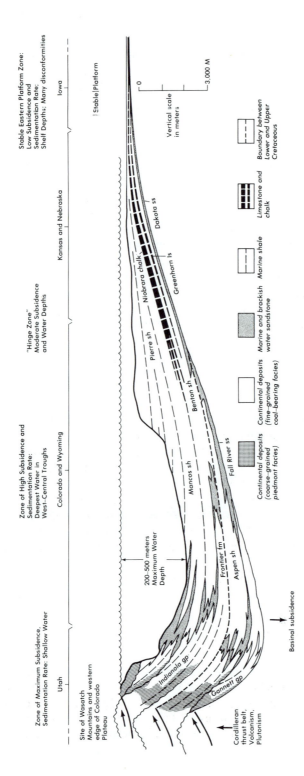

FIG. 3-1 Stratigraphic relations of Cretaceous sedimentary rocks in the U. S. Western Interior. Note the influence of tectonic uplift in the west (especially Utah) on voluminous clastic sedimentation; conversely, few clastic sediments were shed off the eastern, stable platform, so that shales and carbonates were deposited in that area. (After E. G. Kaufmann, 1977 and 1984, with permission of the Geological Association of Canada.)

quence of rocks seen at one particular location provides evidence not only of local depositional environment changes over time at that one particular place but also evidence of lateral environmental variations from place to place within the general region. For example, refer to Fig. 3-1. The Upper Cretaceous rocks exposed in, say, western Colorado indicate a change in depositional environment from offshore marine shales to nearshore marine sands. Moreover, the vertical superposition of the rocks is such that each successive rock stratum, or facies, is the immediate lateral equivalent of the one below and the one above. Furthermore, given the origin of these different facies, we can conclude that this interval of the stratigraphic record on the Colorado Plateau records a regional retreat of the Cretaceous sea. (Why?)*

As we have noted, Walther's law is broadly applicable to stratigraphic intervals that do not contain major breaks in sedimentation, or *unconformities.* A *stratigraphic sequence,* then, can be defined as a vertical succession of rocks genetically related to each other by Walther's law and bounded above and below by unconformities. These unconformities that envelop stratigraphic sequences represent breaks in the stratigraphic record produced either by nondeposition or erosion.

The stratigrapher and geophysicist Peter Vail and his colleagues have used stratigraphic sequence analysis to document coastline advance and retreat through Phanerozoic time. Figure 3-2 shows the results of this analysis, with major relative sea-level fluctuations inferred from stratigraphic sequences on a global scale. An important note regarding this type of analysis is that it yields only *relative* sea-level information; hence, a prograding shoreline may represent either an absolute drop in sea level (for example, resulting from glaciation) or a regional increase in sedimentation (for example, resulting from mountain-building). For this reason, the fine-scale aspects of ancient sea-level change are often controversial. However, the major (first-order) aspects of Phanerozoic sea-level variation, shown in Fig. 3-2, are fairly well accepted.

FACIES MODELS

The genetic approach to environmental stratigraphy, represented by facies analysis, has proved an extremely useful interpretive guide to the stratigraphic record. In this section, we will outline the *environmental processes* and *sedimentary responses* occurring within seven different environmental regimes: fluvial, deltaic, clastic and carbonate tidal flat, carbonate shelf, submarine fan, and deep-water pelagic. For each we will describe the lateral variations in facies and how the facies appear in the stratigraphic record when vertically superimposed on each other. Remember, though, that these are idealized models that are by no means always seen this perfectly in real outcrops. But the models do represent the key sedimen-

---

*Occasionally throughout the book we will ask questions that, with a little thought, you should be able to answer. We do this not to disconcert you, but to encourage you to respond actively to what you are reading.

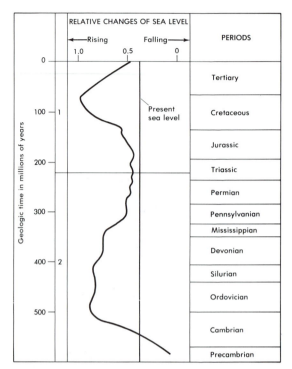

FIG. 3-2 Variation in relative sea level through Phanerozoic time, based on seismic stratigraphic sequence analysis. (From P. R. Vail and others, 1977, reprinted by permission of American Association of Petroleum Geologists.)

tologic and paleontological features abstracted from many specific examples studied by geologists.

Fluvial Facies

One major terrestrial sedimentary environment is the river valley. Most terrestrial erosion occurs by flowing water, and the sediments are carried down streams in river channels, eventually reaching the sea or an inland lake. In the lower reaches of a typical river valley, the river meanders back and forth over the sediments that it has previously deposited. Over time the river erodes and transports this sedimentary material, all the while lowering its longitudinal profile from its headwaters, in the surrounding upland areas, to its mouth, where it empties into a sea or lake.

As shown in Fig. 3-3, there are various sedimentary deposits in the river valley. First, there are the coarse sands and gravels in the channel itself that are part of the river's traction load (refer to page 18). Next, there are the sands deposited on the inside bends of the meandering channel; these are called *point bar deposits*. The river erodes sediment on the opposite, or cut, bank on the outside bend, and it migrates, or meanders, in that direction.

At times of high water the river occasionally rises over its channel banks and floods the adjacent valley. As the rising water leaves the channel, it loses some of

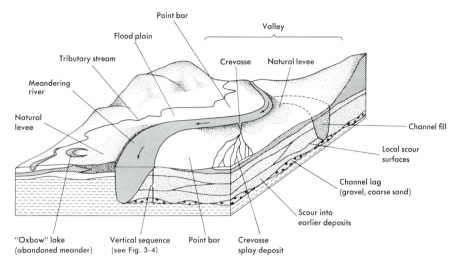

FIG. 3-3 Block diagram of a meandering river valley. The river flows back and forth across its own floodplain, leaving in its wake a vertical sequence of characteristic fluvial facies, which is shown in detail in Fig. 3-4.

its flow velocity and, consequently, deposits sand and silt along the margins of the channel, forming natural levees. The finer-grained, suspended sediment of the floodwaters settles farther out in the valley. Sometimes floodwaters breach a previously formed natural levee and create a small deltalike deposit or *crevasse splay* on the valley floor next to the river channel.

What we have just described is the appearance of the river channel and its sediments at one particular short interval of time. Figure 3-4 shows how the vertical sequence of sediments builds up over time as the meandering river continues to migrate back and forth across the valley. Such vertical sequences of fluvial facies are commonly seen in the stratigraphic record. Note the decrease in overall grain size going up in the sequence, resulting in its being termed a *fining-upward cycle,* because of repeated migrations of the river channel. In addition to changes in sediment grain size, there are also changes in the kinds of primary inorganic structures, especially cross-stratification. Fossils are relatively scarce in such vertical sequences. When they do occur, they include isolated vertebrate bones and teeth, as well as plant fragments.

Deltaic Facies

When a river reaches the sea, its current velocity drops rapidly, and consequently, the sediments carried along by the river's flow are deposited at its mouth. The coarser part of the suspended load, mostly sand, is deposited at the river's mouth just as it enters the sea; the finer-grained portion, mostly mud, drifts farther offshore, where it slowly settles out of suspension. As shown in Fig. 3-5, the ac-

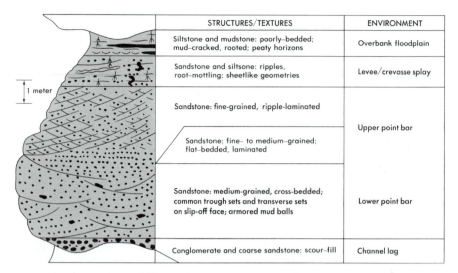

	STRUCTURES/TEXTURES	ENVIRONMENT
	Siltstone and mudstone: poorly-bedded; mud-cracked, rooted; peaty horizons	Overbank floodplain
	Sandstone and siltsone: ripples, root-mottling; sheetlike geometries	Levee/crevasse splay
	Sandstone: fine-grained, ripple-laminated	Upper point bar
	Sandstone: fine- to medium-grained; flat-bedded, laminated	
	Sandstone: medium-grained, cross-bedded; common trough sets and transverse sets on slip-off face; armored mud balls	Lower point bar
	Conglomerate and coarse sandstone: scour-fill	Channel lag

1 meter

FIG. 3-4   Generalized fining-upward cycle of fluvial facies in a meandering river valley. Compare with Fig. 3-3. Why do sediments decrease in grain size upward in the sequence? Why is the sequence cyclic?

FIG. 3-5   Block diagram of a delta. Sand is deposited along the river channel and at its mouth as it enters the sea. Mud accumulates marginal to the channel and in front of the delta. Floods will create levees and crevasse splay deposits. When the deltaic sediments build up to sea level, swamps will form. Compare this with Fig. 3-3, which shows somewhat similar distribution of facies farther up the river channel, away from the river mouth.

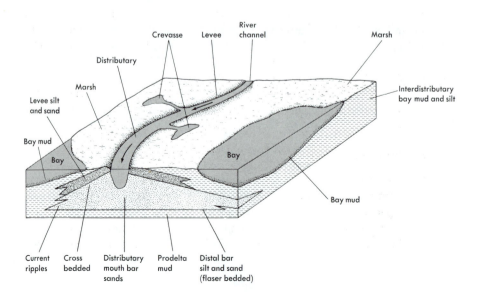

cumulating delta will be laced with long, linear distributary sands that mark successive positions of the river channel. These sands pass laterally into silts and clays away from the river channel. Natural levees will also be present, recording overbank flooding. A marsh or swamp will eventually form where the delta builds up to mean sea level.

Over time the river channel migrates back and forth across the top of its delta, so that a vertical sequence of deltaic facies builds up: offshore marine prodelta muds to distributary channel sands to natural levee and back-swamp muds (Fig. 3-6). When the

FIG. 3-6 Generalized vertical sequence of deltaic facies. Compare with Fig. 3-5. What causes the systematic changes in average grain size and sedimentary structures going upward in the sequence from the prodeltaic environment to the chenier sands and bay muds at the top?

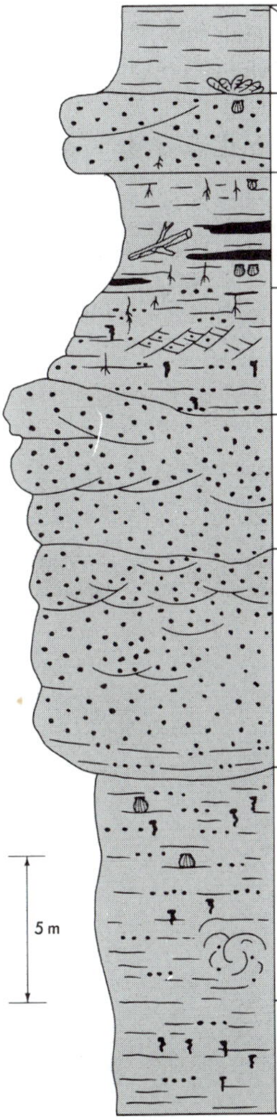

	STRUCTURES/TEXTURES		ENVIRONMENT
	Mudstone: marine; possible oyster reefs		Peridelta marine
	Sandstone: Typical dune and beach features; coarsening upward; shell debris	Destructional	Chenier
	Mudstone: structureless, burrowed, rooted; peaty layers, logs, shells		Swamp and marsh
	Silty sandstone and silty clay: ripple-laminated; organic-rich, burrowed		Natural levee
	Sandstone: fine-to medium-grained, well-sorted, ripple-laminated, cross-bedded; scour and fill, contorted bedding, channel geometries		Distributary channel
	Sandstone and siltstone: better sorting and coarsening upward, wave and current rippled, multidirectional cross-beds; plant debris laminae	Delta constructional phase	Distributary channel mouth bar
	Shaley siltstone: parallel and cross-laminated (upper part); shells, plants, mud clasts common; soft-sediment deformation structures		Delta front
	Silty shale: parallel and lenticular silt laminae common, thinning seaward; abundant fauna and burrowing		Prodelta

river is not actively building one part of its delta (constructional phase), the sea usually attacks and erodes it (destructional phase). The waves and currents rework the deltaic sediments, winnowing out the finer-grained materials and leaving behind the coarser sands, creating a *chenier plain*.

Fossils are fairly common in deltaic facies. Shells and burrows of bottom-dwelling invertebrates are found in the marine muds of the delta front and prodelta facies. Vertebrate remains and plant fragments occur in the deltaic swamp facies.

Clastic Tidal-Flat Facies

Coastal waves and currents rework and redistribute clastic sediments along the shoreline. In regions where there is a large range in tidal level (≥ 1 meter), three distinct sedimentary environments form (Fig. 3-7). Above mean high tide is the *salt marsh* with salt-tolerant vegetation, tidal creeks, and occasional brackish ponds. *Tidal flats* lie between mean high and low water. Marine animals and plants adapted to frequent subaerial exposure flourish here either by burrowing into the tidal-flat

FIG. 3-7 Block diagram showing clastic tidal-flat facies. Periodic flooding and ebbing of the tide moves sediment and water back and forth across the tidal flat. Burrowed muds accumulate in the salt marsh and high part of the tidal flat, while cross-stratified sands are deposited in the lower part of the tidal flat and in the channels and gullies draining the marsh and flat. Migration of the gullies across the flat causes "lateral" sedimentation in the gully; settling out of suspended mud at slack high water results in "vertical" sedimentation on the high flat and salt marsh.

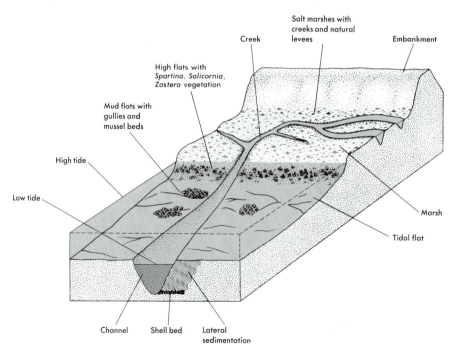

sands and muds or by having the ability to withstand desiccation. The lower part of the flat is crossed by gullies eroded by the ebbing tides. The *subtidal* environment occurs below mean low-tide level and includes not only the organisms and sediments just offshore from the flats but also those within the channels and creeks that remain constantly submerged, whatever the tidal fluctuation.

Reworked shells and mud clasts accumulate in the tidal channels and gullies; depending on the particular environmental conditions, there may also be beds of attached molluscs (mussels or oysters) living there. As the channels and gullies migrate across the tidal flat and marsh, these sediments and organisms move with them. The tidal-flat sediments themselves become finer-grained higher up on the flat, owing to the decreased strength of the flooding and ebbing tidal waters. The lower flat sands display good cross-stratification whose dip reverses itself as the tidal flow changes direction. Higher flat muds show disrupted bedding owing to the burrowing of tidal-flat organisms. The salt-marsh deposits are burrowed muds with abundant plant remains and root casts. The vertical sequence that we have just described is shown in Fig. 3-8. As with all the facies sequences we have discussed, the tidal-flat sequence will recur repeatedly if the area continues to subside and accumulate sediments and if the depositional environments remain the same.

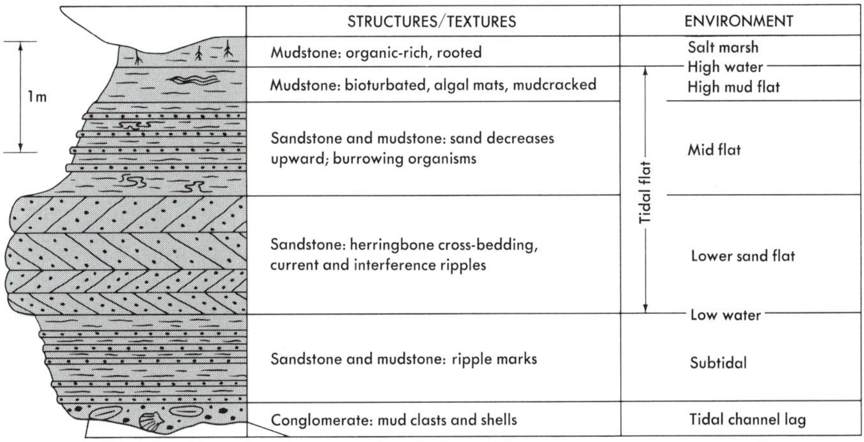

	STRUCTURES/TEXTURES	ENVIRONMENT
	Mudstone: organic-rich, rooted	Salt marsh
		High water
	Mudstone: bioturbated, algal mats, mudcracked	High mud flat
	Sandstone and mudstone: sand decreases upward; burrowing organisms	Mid flat
	Sandstone: herringbone cross-bedding, current and interference ripples	Lower sand flat
		Low water
	Sandstone and mudstone: ripple marks	Subtidal
	Conglomerate: mud clasts and shells	Tidal channel lag

FIG. 3-8 Generalized vertical sequence of clastic tidal-flat sedimentation. Compare with previous figure of tidal-flat environments and account for the changes in fossils, sedimentary structures, and sediment grain size.

Carbonate Tidal-Flat Facies

Along coasts in the warm, low latitudes, where little or no clastic sedimentation occurs, there are well-developed carbonate tidal-flat facies. The sediments are calcareous—calcite and aragonite—because they come from the shelly invertebrates and calcareous algae living there. Evaporation rates tend to be high, so that the sediments are often soon altered and cemented after deposition, owing to solution, precipitation, and replacement of mineral matter from seawater within the sediments.

As shown in Fig. 3-9, carbonate tidal flats have a salt marsh or swamp above normal high tide, mud and sand on the flat between high and low tide, and subtidal, marine sediments below low tide.

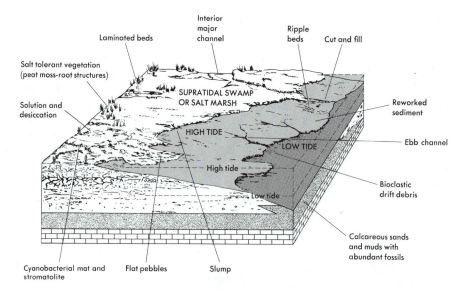

FIG. 3-9   Block diagram of carbonate tidal-flat facies. The horizontal dimension depends on the tidal range and the dip of the depositional surface, varying on the average from tens to thousands of meters. Early cementation, solution/precipitation, and replacement of the calcareous sediments results in their lithification and diagenesis. Subsequent erosion and reworking of the sediment produce clasts that are redeposited, often as limestone-pebble conglomerates along scour surfaces. Cyanobacterial mats in the tidal flat and supratidal marsh trap and bind sediment, building algal stromatolites whose sizes and shapes depend on the strength and frequency of water movement as well as the availability of sediment that can be incorporated in the mats.

Carbonate tidal-flat sediments usually have abundant stromatolites that often show some evidence of subaerial desiccation, mostly polygonal mud cracks. Desiccation and early cementation of these sediments turn them into dense, indurated materials that produce clasts and chips when eroded by strong tides or storm-generated waves. Thus, scour surfaces with limestone-pebble conglomerates are commonly seen in these facies. Winnowed shell beds of marine organisms living in the subtidal environment can be deposited on the tidal flats by strong tides or storm waves. Figure 3-10 shows the typical sequence of sediments seen in a carbonate tidal-flat environment, starting with the nearshore subtidal deposits and going up through the tidal-flat and supratidal (above normal high tide) sediments.

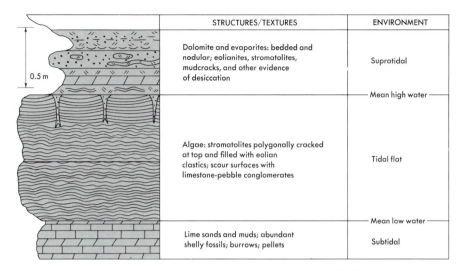

	STRUCTURES/TEXTURES	ENVIRONMENT
	Dolomite and evaporites: bedded and nodular; eolianites, stromatolites, mudcracks, and other evidence of desiccation	Supratidal
		Mean high water
	Algae: stromatolites polygonally cracked at top and filled with eolian clastics; scour surfaces with limestone-pebble conglomerates	Tidal flat
		Mean low water
	Lime sands and muds; abundant shelly fossils; burrows; pellets	Subtidal

FIG. 3-10 Vertical sequence of facies built up in a carbonate tidal-flat environment. Refer to Fig. 3-9 and relate major features of each facies to the individual depositional environments. How does this tidal-flat sequence differ from that formed in a clastic environment as shown in Fig. 3-8?

Reef Facies

In the previous chapter we discussed how flourishing reefs can alter the surrounding patterns of sedimentation. We also indicated how the core of the reef may form a barrier that separates a shallow, quieter water lagoon in the back reef from the deeper, open-sea environment in front of the reef (refer to Fig. 2-11). We can now ask what sort of vertical sequence will form if the area continues to subside and the reef continues to grow faster than the rate of subsidence—a fairly common geologic circumstance.

Using Walther's law, we can predict that the reef barrier will build out over the fore-reef slope deposits, which, in turn, will migrate toward the open ocean. The back-reef lagoon will migrate over the earlier-formed reef-barrier facies. Thus, each facies will cover its lateral equivalent in the seaward direction. The vertical sequence that develops is shown in Fig. 3-11.

Submarine Fans

As mentioned previously, submarine fans are deltalike structures that form in continental-slope and -rise environments; they are usually supplied with sediment from submarine canyons. In some settings, and especially in carbonate slopes, the canyon feeder systems are so closely spaced that individual fans are not recognizable; instead, a base-of-slope apron develops from the coalescing sediment sources. Well-developed submarine fans are more characteristic of clastic slope-and-rise environments than of their carbonate counterparts.

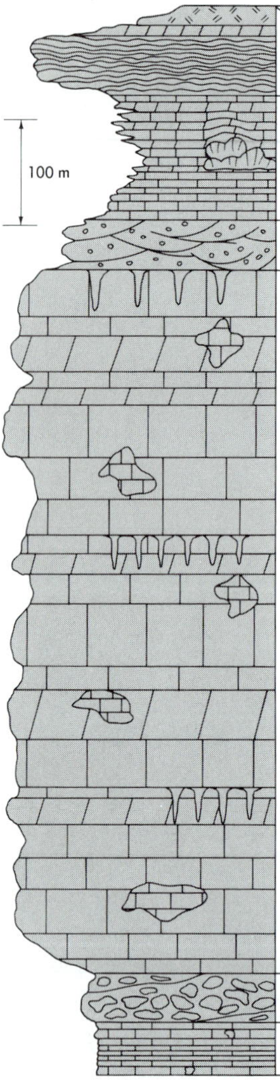

	STRUCTURES/TEXTURES	ENVIRONMENT
	Stromatolitic dolomite and evaporites	Tidal flat
100 m	Lime sandstone and mudstone: pellets and skeletal debris; dolomitization common; local hexacoral patch reefs	Lagoon with some patch reefs
	Oolite: well-sorted and cross-stratified skeletal debris	Inter-reef; back reef
	Reef limestone: may be algal, coralline, crinoidal, etc; large primary and solution voids (exaggerated here), which may be filled with later sediment; dolomitization common; subaerial exposure results in solution of reef rock; nonreef building organisms common	Reef
	Breccia: angular reef rubble	Forereef slope
	Mudstones: dark carbonate, commonly in turbidites; pelagic organisms	Open sea

FIG. 3-11 Vertical sequence of reef facies, going from deep-water, open-sea sediments up through increasingly shallow water sediments into the back-reef lagoon and carbonate tidal-flat facies. Occasional subaerial exposure of the reef core during slightly lowered sea levels results in solution of the reef limestone. Oolite, or rounded grains of calcium carbonate that precipitate from shallow seawater, caps the reef growth. The back-reef lagoon, although also shallow, is a relatively quiet water environment, protected from the full force of the ocean waves by the reef barrier.

A schematic view of a typical submarine fan is presented in Fig. 3-12. A central feeder channel extends across the upper reaches of the fan; within this main channel, very coarse conglomerate is usually present, and slumping is common.

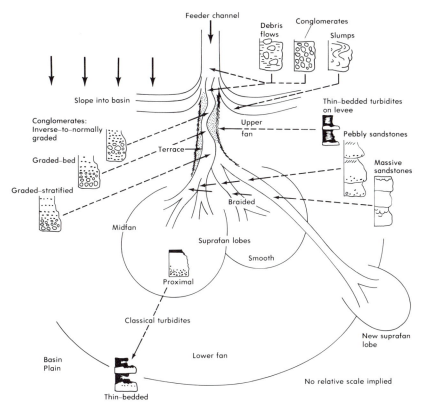

FIG. 3-12 Plan (top) view of generalized submarine fan and associated sedimentary fabrics. (From R. G. Walker, 1979, with permission of the Geological Association of Canada.)

Distally, this stout feeder channel branches into numerous smaller channels. These second-order channels, diagnostic of midfan environments, are sites of massive or pebbly sandstone deposition, whereas the interchannel areas on the suprafan lobes of the midfan are dominated by turbidite deposition. The lower fan lacks channels and preserves thin-bedded turbidites.

Submarine fans, like deltas, usually build seaward through time, so that a generalized stratigraphic sequence for this system has basal, outer-fan lithofacies overlain by midfan lithofacies and finally capped with inner-fan lithofacies (Fig. 3-13). Within this overall progression, some individual facies (outer fan, for example) preserve coarsening-upward fabrics, whereas other facies (inner fan, for example) normally fine upward.

We have stressed lithofacies recognition of ancient submarine fan environments because in most clastic submarine fans, fossils are relatively scarce; hence, biofacies analysis is often not informative. The scarcity of fossils has been commented on by many researchers, who conclude that the very high sedimentation

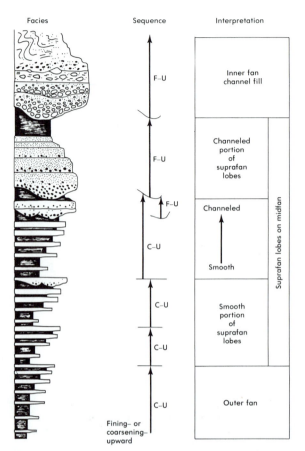

| Facies | Sequence | Interpretation |

FIG. 3-13 Generalized stratigraphic sequence for clastic submarine fan. (From R. G. Walker, 1979, with permission of the Geological Association of Canada.)

Inner fan channel fill — F–U

Channeled portion of suprafan lobes — F–U

Channeled — F–U

Smooth — C–U

Suprafan lobes on midfan

Smooth portion of suprafan lobes — C–U

Outer fan — C–U

Fining– or coarsening– upward

rates may exclude abundant and diverse organisms. In a few instances, as in the California Continental Borderland, insufficient levels of oxygen may also restrict organisms. However, other submarine fans may have trace fossils and even microscopic, planktonic fossils in their finer-grained, more distal parts.

Deep-Sea Pelagic Facies

Pelagic deposits cover an enormous area of the modern ocean floor and are too heterogeneous to be described by a single model. Still, some important generalizations can be made about stratigraphic sequences of pelagic litho- and biofacies in rifted ocean basins. These sedimentological generalizations can often be used to resolve tectonic as well as environmental questions.

A major control on the composition of sediments in the deep sea is the chemistry of the overlying seawater. Especially important is the depth gradient of increasing dissolution of calcium carbonate grains. With increasing depth beneath the surface waters of the ocean, there is an increasing tendency for carbonate grains to dissolve in the surrounding seawater. This dissolution occurs because the increasing pressure and decreasing temperature with greater depth allow more carbon dioxide to dissolve in seawater, thereby making the seawater more acidic. This carbon dioxide gradient steepens appreciably at intermediate depths in the water column and thus creates a zone of rapidly increasing dissolution, called the *lysocline* (Fig. 3-14). At depths of 3,500 to 4,500 meters, a point is reached where the rate of supply of calcareous skeletal material from above is equal to the rate of dissolution of calcite. This level is called the *calcite compensation depth (CCD)*; beneath this depth, isolated carbonate particles may be preserved, but significant thicknesses of carbonate sediment will not accumulate. Also, what little calcite does reach the seafloor is quickly etched by further dissolution.

Figure 3-15 illustrates the relationship between subsidence of the rifted oceanic crust and deposition of carbonate versus noncarbonate sediment. The relationship is particularly clear for fast-spreading ridges, shown on the upper diagram, where carbonate oozes are deposited on relatively young oceanic crust near the ridge axis. As the oceanic crust cools, it becomes denser and subsides, and the seafloor then passes below the CCD, so that only siliceous deposits will be

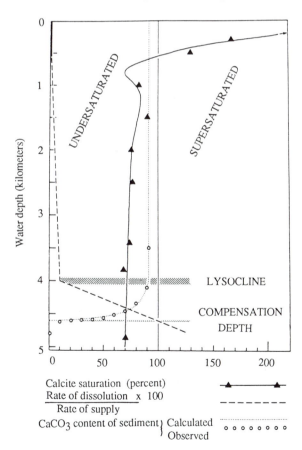

FIG. 3-14 Profile of calcite saturation (triangles) versus calcite dissolution (dashed line) with depth in the tropical Pacific Ocean. The lysocline is the zone in the water column in which dissolution of calcite increases greatly (indicated by cross-hatching). The resulting $CaCO_3$ content of the sediment is indicated by circles. (From T. Van Andel, 1974, and J. Kennett, 1982.)

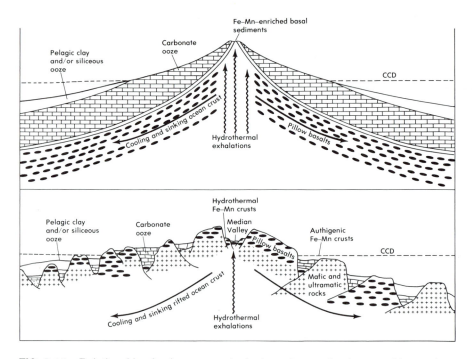

FIG. 3-15 Relationship of calcareous pelagic deposits to axis of ocean ridge and to the level of the calcite compensation depth (CCD). *Upper diagram:* facies relationships on a fast-spreading ridge such as the East Pacific Rise. (From T. A. Davies and D. S. Gorsline, 1976.) *Lower diagram:* facies relationships on a slow-spreading ridge such as the Mid-Atlantic Ridge. (From R. E. Garrison, 1974.)

preserved. Thus, the typical sedimentary sequence above oceanic crust involves a thin zone of iron- and manganese-enriched sediments immediately above the ridge-formed basalts, which is overlain by carbonate ooze composed of pelagic skeletal material. This zone is in turn overlain by pelagic clay or siliceous pelagic skeletal material. In slowly spreading ridges the overall vertical sequence is generally the same, but the geometry of the units may be more irregular (see lower diagram of Fig. 3-15).

SEISMIC STRATIGRAPHY AND DEPOSITIONAL SYSTEMS

One of the most powerful methods for recognition of stratigraphic sequences is *seismic-reflection profiling.* Unlike the visual analysis of outcrops we discussed previously, *seismic stratigraphy* uses remote geophysical techniques to identify and correlate stratigraphic units. In seismic-reflection profiling a sound source emits an acoustic signal that penetrates subsurface layers of sediment or rock; the sound is reflected by the various sediment or rock layers, and the returning signal is received by an instrument (in marine research, by a hydrophone) that measures the time elapsed between the outgoing sound and the incoming echoes (Fig. 3-16). Reflections from sedimentary units in the shallow subsurface are received more quickly than those from deeper strata, so the resulting seismic profile records both the vertical order and relative thickness of subsurface stratigraphic sequences. The individual reflectors that make up the profile are generated by variations in density and sonic velocity in the sediments and rocks beneath the earth's surface. Thus, only where stratigraphic contacts correspond to significant changes in physical properties will seismic reflections correspond to individual bedding surfaces.

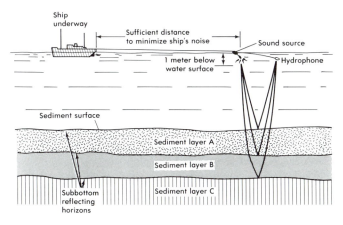

FIG. 3-16   Marine seismic-profiling method, in which a device emitting an acoustic signal is towed behind a ship; a receiver (hydrophone) collects echoes reflected from subsurface strata. (From J. B. Hersey, in *The Sea* (M. N. Hill, ed.). Copyright © 1963, John Wiley. Reprinted by permission of John Wiley and Sons.)

Unconformities frequently show up very well in seismic profiles because of the varying physical properties of sediments below and above. Different depositional systems also have contrasting seismic signatures; for example, a reef will yield very different seismic facies than a prograding deltaic sequence. Figure 3-17 shows how seismic profiles can be used to differentiate glacial from lacustrine sediments in a lake formed during Pleistocene glaciation.

Seismic stratigraphy provides a tool for identifying and continuously correlating stratigraphic sequences on a grand scale; this method can document sedimentary sections whose thicknesses and lateral extents greatly exceed those of outcrops. The seismic stratigraphic sections shown in Figs. 3-17 and 3-18 represent thicknesses of many tens of meters; some seismic profiles, though, may penetrate kilometers or—in exceptional cases—tens of kilometers. Thus, far greater intervals of Earth history can be analyzed in an individual seismic section than can be seen in most outcrops. The scientific trade-off is that one cannot visually examine the sedimentary strata in

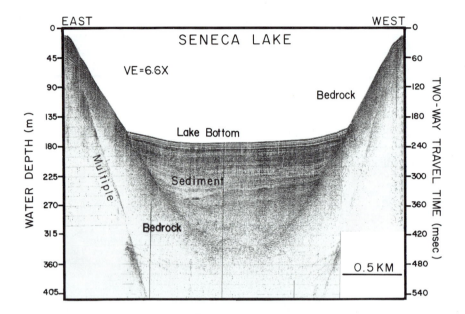

FIG. 3-17 Seismic-reflection profile through Seneca Lake, central New York. Seneca is one of the Finger Lakes, formed during Pleistocene glaciation. Note that the lake bottom reflector forms a broad U shape but that the bedrock surface is more of a V shape. The irregular reflectors in the lake center just above bedrock at travel times of 320 to 360 milliseconds are probably late Pleistocene subglacial lake sediments, and the extremely even reflectors in the uppermost part of the sediment correspond to Holocene lake sedimentation. (Profile courtesy of Henry Mullins.)

seismic profiles unless there are cores or boreholes from sites along the profile. Such cores or boreholes also provide the "ground truth" necessary to establish the age of sediments that one has correlated seismically. Only if the ages of seismic sequences are well constrained by core or borehole data can seismic stratigraphy provide a firm basis for regional or global correlations of stratigraphic sequences.

SUMMARY

Sedimentary facies are lateral variations in sediments caused by the localized environmental conditions within a depositional basin. As these local environments oscillate and migrate through geologic time, sedimentary facies attain three-dimensional configurations. A vertical succession of genetically linked sedimentary facies is called a stratigraphic sequence; such sequences are bounded by erosional or nondepositional surfaces known as unconformities. Walther's law, a key generalization about stratigraphic sequences, states that unless there is a break in sedimentation (unconformity), only those facies deposited in laterally adjacent environments may succeed one another vertically in the stratigraphic record.

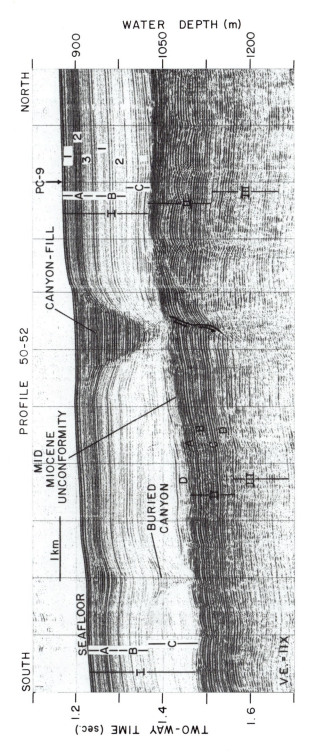

FIG. 3-18 Seismic-reflection profile along the west Florida continental slope, illustrating a mid-Miocene unconformity that separates seismic stratigraphic sequence I (above) from sequence II and III (below). Note the buried and infilled canyons that formed in this continental slope environment. A slump surface also offsets sediments in the middle portion of the profile. (Profile courtesy of Henry Mullins.)

55

A genetic approach to sedimentary facies emphasizes the relationship between local environmental processes and resulting environmental responses. We have discussed facies models for seven distinctive sedimentary environments that form a large fraction of ancient stratigraphic sequences: fluvial, deltaic, clastic tidal flat, carbonate tidal flat, carbonate shelf, submarine fan, and deep-water pelagic environment. Many other sedimentary environments also exist and are represented in the stratigraphic record. For all depositional environments, the accumulation of sedimentary facies reflects an interplay between the physical, chemical, and biological features of the environment, the tectonics of the sedimentary basin, and fluctuations in global sea level.

In addition to outcrop-scale documentation of sedimentary sequences, seismic stratigraphy provides a way of examining thick sections of subsurface sedimentary rocks. Biostratigraphic dating of wells and cores can calibrate the ages of subsurface sediments correlated using seismic techniques. Using both seismic and outcrop data, we can use regional and global patterns of stratigraphic sequences to test new hypotheses about tectonism and global variations in sea level.

4

ORGANISMS
AND ENVIRONMENTS

In solving ecological problems we are concerned with what animals do . . . as whole, living animals, not as dead animals or a series of parts of animals. We study the circumstances under which they do things and . . . the limiting factors which prevent them from doing certain other things. (Charles Elton. 1927. Animal Ecology. *New York: Macmillan, 34.)*

The abundance and wide diversity of fossil organisms show that ancient environments and biotas were dynamic ecological systems, similar in many ways to modern ecosystems. Thus, in part, paleoecologists seek to discover the ecological context in which these fossil organisms fed, moved about, sought shelter, and reproduced. However, ancient and modern ecosystems are not exactly comparable because extinct organisms are not represented in the modern biosphere. Moreover, successions of fossils within the stratigraphic record reflect far longer time spans than those observed in modern ecological studies.

In this chapter we will consider the different influences on the shape and size of organisms and the ecological responses of modern animals and plants to variable physical and chemical environmental factors, including temperature, light, oxygen, carbon dioxide, salinity, turbulence, and substrate. We will then examine some key biological controls on the distribution of modern organisms.

FUNCTIONAL MORPHOLOGY

One of the most striking aspects of an organism's form, or *morphology,* is the relationship between form and function. The study of this relationship, *functional morphology,* can sometimes be applied to analysis of fossils and can be useful in inferring feeding, locomotion, or reproduction in extinct organisms.

For example, the skeletal appendages of various vertebrates are clearly related to the locomotory functions they serve in water, on land, or in the air (Fig. 4-1). Fish have short and broad appendages with a relatively large surface area for moving through the dense medium of water. Land-dwelling vertebrates have longer and narrower limbs for supporting the body in walking and running. In the case of those groups that have returned to the sea (ichthyosauran and plesiosauran reptiles and whales), the limbs have been modified once more and are stubbier and more spatulate than those of related terrestrial groups. Flying vertebrates—the birds, bats, and pterosauran reptiles—have a limb that, when covered with feathers or a skin membrane, forms an aerodynamically stable structure. The crucial point is that despite the different bone configurations characteristic of each evolutionary group, limbs modified for similar functions have similar overall geometries; hence, for many vertebrate appendages, form can be used to interpret function.

An illustration of the utility of functional morphology in invertebrate paleoecological analysis comes from larval shell morphology. Most marine snails

FIG. 4-1 Structure of various vertebrate forelimbs showing the arrangement of homologous bones. Each limb is specifically adapted for a particular way of life, whether burrowing (mole), flying (bat, bird), swimming (whale, icthyosaur, plesiosaur), running (dog, deer, horse), or manipulating objects and tools (human). Various forelimb bones include: humerus, stippled; radius, dark gray; ulna, black; carpals (wrist bones) and phalanges (finger bones), light gray; numbers refer to homologous digits (fingers).

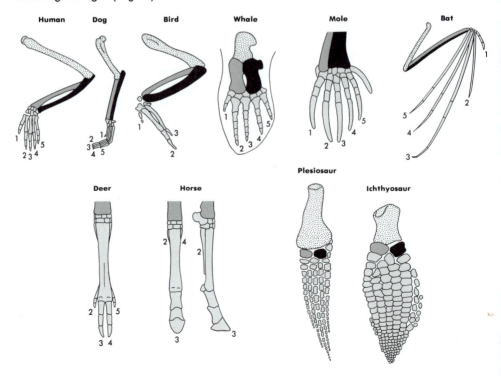

and clams produce *veliger larvae* that represent a discrete developmental phase intermediate between the earliest molluscan larval phase (trochophore) and metamor-
phosis into an adult mollusc. This veliger larva may be either benthic or planktonic;
if planktonic, the larva either may be supplied with a yolky sac from which it feeds
or, alternatively, may feed upon other members of the planktonic community. The
form of the molluscan shell reflects the feeding type of the veliger larva. As Fig. 4-2
illustrates, yolk-feeding gastropod larvae are equipped with a larval shell that is
large in diameter, whereas plankton feeding larvae within the same family have a
smaller-diameter shell. This difference in form and function among larval shells is a
fundamental one, for plankton-feeding larvae can reside for a long time (generally 2
to 6 weeks) in the plankton and may disperse over long distances, but yolk-feeding
larvae, dependent on a limited and internal food supply, normally settle to the bottom after only a few days; thus, individual yolk-feeding larvae are not so widely
dispersed. This contrast in larval residence time among the plankton may ultimately
result in broader geographic distribution for those molluscan species that have
plankton-feeding larvae, a premise that can be tested for many fossil taxa.

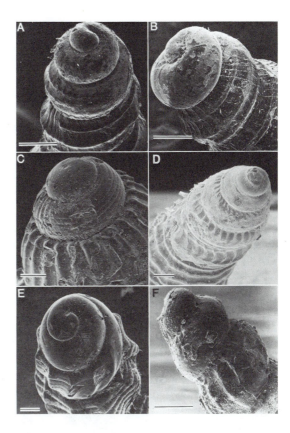

FIG. 4-2 Larval shell
morphology of some Late
Cretaceous gastropods. A,
D, and F are plankton
feeders; note small initial
diameter of the apex of the
shell. B, C, and E are yolk
feeders; observe that these
have very broad, robust shell
apices. Scale bar equals 100
microns. (From D. Jablonski,
1986, *Bull. Mar. Sci.* 39(2):
573.)

Clearly, however, there are many aspects of form that cannot be explained by functional interpretation alone. We must also consider the overall body plan and skeletal material with which a given organism has to work, and we must be aware of environmentally imposed variation on "ideal" body plans.

CONSTRUCTIONAL MORPHOLOGY

Organisms are not infinitely plastic in the sense of being able to construct the "ideal" solution to functional problems; they are limited by their symmetry, their skeletal building materials (mineralogy and crystal form), their growth rate and size, as well as many other factors. In other words, organisms in general, like human carpenters, are limited by their blueprints and by the materials at hand. The field of *constructional morphology* investigates those elements of organic form that are most appropriately interpreted as constructional rather than purely functional in origin.

ECOPHENOTYPIC VARIATION IN MORPHOLOGY

Variable environments may produce morphological variation in organisms that is expressed morphologically in the phenotype but not genetically in the genotype. In other words, some variation in form can be attributed to ecological but not genetic differences among or between groups of organisms, hence the term *ecophenotypic variation.* A sun-loving plant may flourish near a west-facing window or may remain small and spindly near a north-facing window. Similarly, the common Eastern oyster, *Crassostrea virginica,* grows best when the surrounding seawater averages 15°C; above and below this temperature, growth yields decline (Table 4-1).

Table 4-1 Temperature as Related to Growth and Form

	Mean Annual Temp. (°C)	Average No. of Growing Months	Yield per Bushel	Yield per Growing Month
Canada	6	46	120	2.6
Long Island Sound	10	36	120	3.4
Chesapeake Bay	15	24	96	4.0
South Carolina	20	30	76	2.5
Gulf of Mexico	22	30	72	2.4

Size and growth rates of *Crassostrea virginica* along the eastern coast of North America
(After P. Butler, 1953.)

Such ecophenotypic variation is common among modern faunas and floras and has been recognized in the fossil record as well. A particularly frequent expression of ecophenotypic variation is that of variation in size, although ornamental

FIG. 4-3 Ecophenotypic variation in the Permian scallop *Guizhoupecten cheni willisensis* from West Texas. All specimens natural size (× 1). (From N. D. Newell and D. W. Boyd, 1985, courtesy of *American Museum Novitates,* no. 2831, 1985.)

variability is also common (as in Fig. 4-3, a scallop from the Permian rocks of North America). The key to recognition of this phenomenon is that individuals of approximately the same biological age have perceptibly different morphologies that can be related to identifiable environmental factors.

PHYSICAL AND CHEMICAL ENVIRONMENTAL FACTORS

The distribution and abundance (as well as ecophenotypic variation of form) of modern organisms can be related to both physical and chemical environmental factors and to biological controls. We will summarize the effects on organisms of some of the most critical physical and chemical influences of environments; then in the following section we will focus on biological factors that limit the distribution and abundance of modern organisms.

This review is intended to be a general summary of individual limiting factors. Remember that these factors normally interact with one another, so that the overall impact of the environment on organisms is often far greater than the sum of the individual components.

Temperature

One of the most important physical environmental variables is the *temperature* of the surrounding medium. Both the absolute temperature and the range of temperatures to which the organism is subjected are significant, because most organisms (with the significant exceptions of birds and mammals) are only weakly able to control their internal temperature relative to the ambient temperatures.

As the internal temperature of an organism varies, so do the reaction rates of many physiological processes; thus, metabolism, development, and reproduction ordinarily fluctuate with environmental temperature change. This covariance of biological reaction rates with temperature is summarized by *van't Hoff's rule,* which states that for every 10°C of temperature increase, biological reaction rates increase by a factor of 1 to 6 (this numerical factor is generally called the Q_{10} constant for a given species). Although exceptions to the rule do occur, this acceleration in biological rates with increasing temperature is a general phenomenon (Fig. 4-4). Note, however, that for most organisms there is a thermal turning point above which continued temperature increase is deleterious. Figure 4-4 illustrates the thermal responses of an intertidal limpet, for which this thermal turning point is 30°C in water and 25°C in air.

Besides these direct influences on physiological reactions, temperature variations have indirect effects that may be equally important from an ecological perspective. The solubility of many solids in fresh water or seawater varies as a function of temperature, so that nutrient availability may co-vary with temperature. Conversely, the solubility of gases such as oxygen and carbon dioxide decreases with increasing temperature. Thus, temperature affects not only an organism's respiratory requirements but also the absolute amount of dissolved oxygen available for consumption.

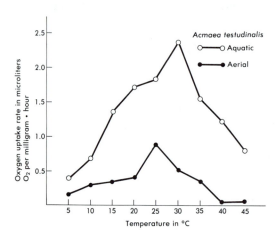

FIG. 4-4 Respiration rates of the intertidal limpet *Acmaea testudinalis* in response to increasing temperature in seawater (open circles) versus air (filled circles). (From R. F. McMahon and W. D. Russell-Hunter, 1977.)

Light

Sunlight is the basic energy source for nearly all the earth's ecosystems. Solar energy fuels photosynthesis, the process by which plants convert carbon dioxide and water into various organic molecules (most notably carbohydrates but also fatty acids and proteins). The storage of chemical energy by plants during photosynthesis and its release by plants and animals during respiration are summarized by the general equation

$$\text{Energy from solar radiation} + 6CO_2 + 6H_2O \underset{\text{respiration}}{\overset{\text{photosynthesis}}{\rightleftharpoons}} \underset{\text{sugar}}{C_6H_{12}O_6} + 6O_2$$

Respiration, the breakdown of organic molecules formed during photosynthesis, is the major energy source for the plants themselves as well as for consumers that prey upon the plants. Therefore, the intensity and duration of solar energy influx are of central importance to both terrestrial and marine ecosystems.

The amount and duration of solar radiation vary greatly over the earth's surface. Because the earth's axis of daily rotation is inclined, solar energy in mid- and high latitudes varies markedly on a seasonal basis. Whereas plants in the tropics receive strong light for about 12 hours each day of the year, plants in higher latitudes receive light that is much less intense and much more unevenly distributed.

In aqueous environments, the distribution of light varies vertically as well as laterally. In marine environments the intensity of light decreases very rapidly with depth, so that the photic zone (Fig. 1-4) rarely extends beyond 200 meters and may frequently be much shallower. It is estimated that in most marine environments 80 percent of all solar radiation is absorbed in the upper 10 meters of the water column. Not only does the amount of radiation decrease rapidly with water depth, but the wavelength (or color) of the light changes as well. Algae use those wavelengths and intensities of light that are available at different vertical depths in the ocean, so that green algae often are found in the shallowest depths, brown algae at intermediate depths, and red algae in the deeper parts of the photic zone. It is important to underscore, however, that the distribution of these organisms is related not only to wavelength and light intensity but also to other environmental factors, such as temperature and salinity.

Light, like temperature, is an environmental factor that can be harmful at excessively high levels because of the destructive effect of ultraviolet radiation and the degradation of chlorophyll molecules through photooxidation. This phenomenon, called *photoinhibition,* is well known in phytoplankton populations and is illustrated in Fig. 4-5.

Nutrients

The supply of some elements, such as nitrogen and phosphorus, may limit the growth of phytoplankton in many marine environments as well as in lakes. These elements, together with silica, magnesium, potassium, calcium, and carbon, are

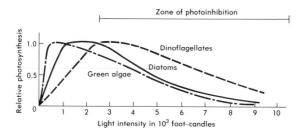

FIG. 4-5 Response of three major phytoplankton groups to increasing light intensities; note zone of photoinhibition at high light intensities. (From T. R. Parsons and others, 1977.)

called *macronutrients* because they are necessary in relatively large quantities to support the prolific growth of phytoplankton. Some other elements, including iron, manganese, copper, zinc, boron, sodium, molybdenum, chlorine, vanadium, and cobalt must also be present, but in much smaller amounts; hence, these have been labeled *micronutrients* or *trace elements.*

For both macro- and micronutrients, phytoplankton growth depends not only on the absolute quantities of these elements but also on seasonal rates of supply. Extreme variations in the abundance of nutrients may lead to "boom-bust" cycles in the plankton, in which the rapid growth of plankton causes depletion of nutrients, which leads to plankton mortality, in turn causing widespread starvation among plankton-feeders. The long-term stability and diversity of an ecosystem may thus be influenced by the constancy or variation of nutrient supply. Shallow-water coral reefs, for example, cannot withstand extreme fluctuations in nutrient availability; reefs are most abundant in habitats with low, but very stable, supplies of nitrogen and phosphorus.

Carbon Dioxide and Oxygen

Two atmospheric gases, carbon dioxide and oxygen, are essential for photosynthesis and respiration in higher organisms; hence, the abundance of these two gases in the atmosphere and water column imposes a major control on the abundance and distribution of organisms.

Carbon dioxide, besides being necessary for photosynthetic organisms, is also ecologically important because it influences the pH, or alkalinity/acidity, of natural waters. When carbon dioxide dissolves in water, it forms the weak acid, carbonic acid, which in turn dissociates to form hydrogen ions and bicarbonate ions. An increase in the carbon dioxide content in marine or fresh water has the ultimate effect of raising the solubility of calcium carbonate. Thus, the amount of carbon dioxide in marine environments partially controls the level of the calcite compensation depth (CCD) in the world ocean; a global increase in carbon dioxide production (by burning of fossil fuels, for example) would ultimately cause a shallowing of the CCD, so that the skeletal remains of calcium carbonate-secreting organisms would be dissolved at shallower depths than in the present ocean. (How would that affect the kinds of sediment preserved at those depths?)

Oxygen is essential for the cellular respiration of most organisms, except for a few groups such as anaerobic bacteria. Because the "biocombustion" of organic molecules produced in photosynthesis requires oxygen, any substantial variation in oxygenation may have a marked effect on biological diversity. This effect is most evident in aqueous environments, where the decay of organic matter produced by planktonic and nektonic organisms in surface waters usually depletes oxygen at intermediate depths in the water column. In the ocean this phenomenon is very widespread and is usually known as the *oxygen-minimum zone* (Fig. 4-6). Note that beneath this zone there is generally a slight increase in oxygenation, owing to deep-ocean circulation, which brings oxygen-rich, polar surface water downward to reoxygenate the oxygen-poor water lying beneath intermediate depths at lower latitudes.

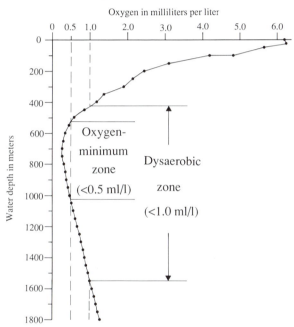

FIG. 4-6 Dissolved oxygen concentrations (milliliters per liter) versus water depth for the central California continental margin. (From J. B. Thompson, H. T. Mullins, C. R. Newton, and T. L. Vercoutere, 1985.)

The biological effects of oxygen depletion in marine environments are often striking. Figure 4-7 illustrates the decline in abundance of major invertebrate groups across a modern oxygen-minimum zone off Point Sur, central California. Note especially the reduction in total density of organisms within the low-oxygen zone. In addition to open-ocean marine environments, many restricted basins, such as the Black Sea and Norwegian fjords, may be permanently or episodically anoxic, limiting the occurrence of many or most marine organisms.

Salinity

In aquatic environments the total amount of dissolved substances, or *salinity,* is an important environmental factor. Streams, rivers, ponds, and lakes differ from oceanic waters in that they are less saline, and they generally have different propor-

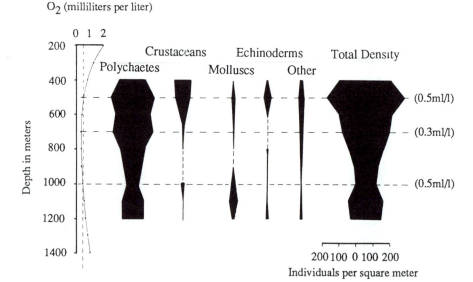

FIG. 4-7 Variation in abundance and density of major invertebrate groups across the oxygen-minimum zone on the continental slope off Point Sur, central California. (From J. B. Thompson, H. T. Mullins, C. R. Newton, and T. L. Vercoutere, 1985.)

tions of individual salts. Thus, although the oceans usually contain 3 to 4 percent of salts in solution, river waters average 0.01 percent and vary from less than 0.001 to 1 percent (a factor of 1,000). In seawater, chloride, sodium, magnesium, sulfate, calcium, and potassium ions constitute approximately 99 percent of the dissolved salts. In contrast, in river water, the most important ions are bicarbonate, calcium, silica, sulfate, chloride, sodium, magnesium, and potassium. In seawater the major dissolved constituent is sodium chloride—hence the "salty" taste of ocean water—and in river water it is calcium carbonate. The depletion of dissolved calcium carbonate in seawater is mainly a consequence of the uptake of calcium and carbonate by organisms in the construction of their calcareous skeleton.

The principal effect of salinity on aquatic organisms is *osmotic pressure.* The cells of organisms are basically viscous chemical solutions within a membrane that is only partially permeable, allowing only water and certain small ions to pass back and forth. The movement of water between cells and the external environment through this semipermeable membrane is called *osmosis.* If the salinity of the internal cell fluids differs from that of the surrounding water, water pressure is directly proportional to the difference in salinity between the two. If the cell's salinity is *less* than that of the surrounding medium, water tends to leave the cell; if, on the other hand, the cell's salinity is *greater,* water tends to enter the cell. The organism must be able to regulate its osmotic pressure if it is to survive in a medium of contrasting salinity; otherwise its cells will be dehydrated or flooded to bursting.

Salinity is relatively constant within most of the world's ocean, with a mean value of 35 parts per thousand dissolved salts. However, in coastal zones at the mouths of rivers or estuaries there may be a marked salinity range from fresh to brackish to fully marine waters. In such environments there is usually a reduction in marine species diversity paralleling the salinity decline shoreward (Fig. 4-8).

Water Energy

Hydraulic energy is another important ecological factor in aqueous environments. Energy from waves, tides, or currents helps bring increased supplies of food, nutrients, and oxygen into the environment for organisms; for stationary organisms

FIG. 4-8 Salinities in the Baltic Sea decrease markedly from the North Sea toward the Gulf of Finland. Paralleling this salinity decrease is a sharp decline in the numbers of species of marine animals. The changes in salinity are due to the freshening of the Baltic Sea by heavy runoff from the surrounding land. (Data from S. G. Segersträle, 1957.)

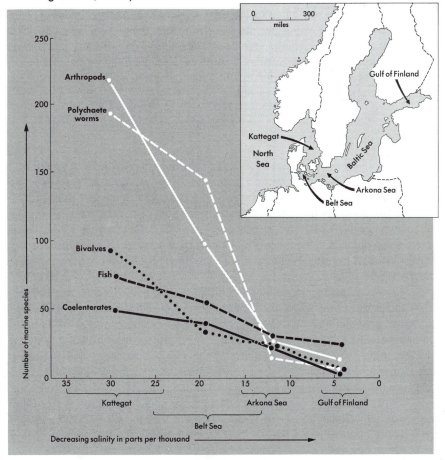

this increased volume of water may appreciably increase growth rates. Water energy also disperses larvae and carries off toxic metabolic wastes. Excessive turbulence may prove harmful if burrowing organisms are exhumed or, conversely, if organisms resting upon or cemented to the substrate are buried by sediment.

Water energy also affects organisms indirectly by controlling the grain size of sediments that accumulate on the substrate. The smaller grains settle out in quieter water, whereas in more turbulent water larger grains are carried in suspension or moved along the bottom (refer to Fig. 2-2). By controlling the size and density of particles able to settle out, hydraulic energy also influences other sedimentary properties such as quantity of organic matter (an important food source for many organisms), porosity, permeability, and sorting. These last three physical properties affect the rate at which organisms can burrow into the sediment or live interstitially among sediment grains (in the case of minute sediment-dwellers).

Marine biologists have also noted that variations in the shape of some shallow-water invertebrates relate to different levels of hydraulic energy in the local environment. For example, in very shallow tropical waters, the stinging coral *Millepora* grows as an encrusting, hummocky colony, whereas in deeper waters, where turbulence is reduced, the colonies assume a vertically bladed, labyrinthine shape. However, for most organisms a direct relationship between water energy and morphology has not been well established, so that in most cases such interpretations are difficult to apply to the fossil record.

Substrate

Most organisms require a surface, or substrate, upon which they pass their lives feeding, seeking mates, avoiding predators, and resting. The need for a substrate is shared by most animals, plants, fungi, and bacteria, as well as most protists. This generalization applies not only to strictly benthic organisms but also to many swimming organisms that feed on the bottom, as well as to many flying organisms in terrestrial habitats. Examples of substrate specificity are particularly striking among plants, which often prefer soils with just the right nitrogen content, moisture, and grain size.

Marine organisms also reflect the influence of substrate. Many invertebrates need either a hard substrate where they can cement or rest freely or a soft substrate into which they can burrow. Figure 4-9 illustrates the wide range of substrate requirements of marine bivalves, reflecting a very broad diversity of living habits, from the rock-boring pholad bivalves to the cemented oysters and burrowing quahog or cherrystone clam. A further, important point is that larval and juvenile organisms may have substrate preferences that are often quite different from those of the adults. Corals, for instance, have planula larvae that can settle only on hard substrates, so that even though the mature coral may be able to rest on a sandy substrate, the initial larval settlement is on a hard substrate, such as a rock surface or piece of gravel or shell.

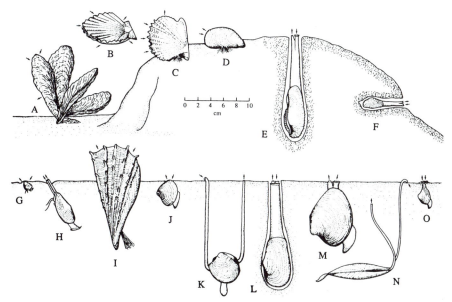

FIG. 4-9 Substrate relations of some modern bivalves. (a)–(d) Surface-dwelling, suspension-feeding bivalves: (a) *Crassostrea*, a cementer; (b) *Pecten*, a bivalve capable of short pulses of swimming; (c), (d) *Pinctada* (pearl oyster) and *Mytilus* (mussel), moored to the substrate by organic threads. (e)–(o) Bivalves living within rock or sediment substrates: (e) *Pholas*, a rock-borer; (f) *Hiatella*, a rock nestler; (g), (h) *Nucula* and *Yoldia*, shallow-burrowing deposit feeders; (i) *Atrina*, a semiinfaunal bivalve; (j) *Astarte*, a shallow infaunal burrower; (k) *Phacoides*, a deeper infaunal bivalve; (l) *Mya*, a relatively deep infaunal suspension feeder; (m) *Mercenaria*, a shallow infaunal suspension feeder; (n) *Tellina*, infaunal deposit feeder; and (o) *Cuspidaria*, an infaunal carnivore. (From J. W. Valentine, 1973, after S. M. Stanley, 1968.)

Burrowing organisms, in particular, must contend with the physical and chemical properties of the sediment they inhabit. One group of burrowing organisms that has been studied extensively is the callianassid crustaceans. These shrimplike organisms inhabit shallow marine environments, where they excavate large burrow systems with diagnostic, 120°-angle branches (Fig. 4-10). Because various *Callianassa* species inhabit different substrates, burrow linings vary according to substrate type. In sandy habitats, where the loose substrate requires that burrows be structurally reinforced, burrow walls are packed with pellets from the organism; in contrast, within firmer substrates the callianassid burrow wall has a grooved texture, and in soft muds the burrow wall is quite smooth.

Figure 4-11 illustrates the relationships of the substrate with other ecological variables, such as the topography, hydrography, and water energy of Great Bahama Bank. Note especially the close correspondence between sediments and bottom communities in this shallow, subtropical, marine environment. The composition of the bottom-dwelling invertebrate communities is strongly influenced not only by the

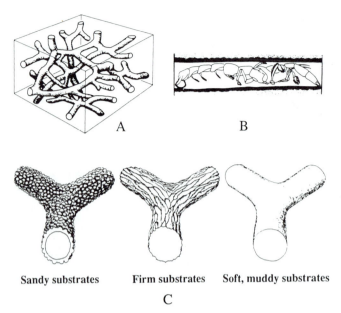

FIG. 4-10 (A) Burrows of callianassid shrimp, showing branching burrow network, (B) ghost shrimp *Callianassa major* inside burrow, and (C) relationship between burrow-wall morphology and sediment type. (A, C from A. A. Ekdale, R. G. Bromley, and S. G. Pemberton, 1984; (B) from R. W. Frey, 1975, reprinted by permission of Springer-Verlag.)

substrate itself but also by associated environmental factors, chiefly water energy and salinity.

Substrate is of enormous importance in paleoecology and environmental stratigraphy because, of all the environmental factors we have discussed, substrate type is the only one that is *directly* preservable in the stratigraphic record. Normally the substrate of the environment becomes the sedimentary rock matrix with little postdepositional alteration beyond compaction, cementation, and recrystallization (see Chapter 5). In contrast, other physical-chemical factors, such as temperature, salinity, and oxygen and nutrient content can often be reconstructed, but these reconstructions are based on *indirect* evidence, either geochemical, paleontological, or sedimentologic.

BIOLOGICAL FACTORS

In addition to physical and chemical environmental factors, biological interactions also limit the distribution and abundance of organisms. Foremost among biological controls are the feeding, or *trophic*, relationships among different organisms. These trophic relationships include the food-gathering mechanisms of individual organisms, predator-prey interactions, symbiosis, and energy flow on the larger scale of entire food chains and webs. Because most plants manufacture their own trophic resources by photosynthesizing, the classification that follows emphasizes animal feeding.

1. **Herbivores** consume plant matter. These include such disparate animals as cattle, which graze on grasses; snails that browse on the algal films on rocky intertidal surfaces; insects and hummingbirds that feed on the nectar of flowering plants; and rodents that eat grains and nuts.

2. **Carnivores** prey on living animals; the prey selected by carnivores may themselves be either herbivorous or carnivorous. Animals such as lions, sharks, and eagles are obviously carnivorous. Also included in this trophic category are many other species whose feeding mechanisms are generally less familiar: these include starfish, cone snails, and shrews. Corals are also considered "microcarnivores," because, despite their tiny size, individual coral polyps ensnare still smaller prey in the water column. Carrion feeders, which prey upon recently killed organisms, are considered carnivores; the vulture falls into this category.

3. **Deposit feeders** feed on the organic debris and detritus on or within the substrate. Within this group are the *selective* deposit feeders, which discriminate between certain kinds of organic matter and avoid ingesting unsuitable elements in the substrate, and *nonselective* deposit feeders, which ingest large quantities of the substrate. Nonselective deposit feeders feed upon large numbers of unicellular algae, bacteria, and other microorganisms as well as organic molecules and tidbits of decomposing animal and plant tissue; they then excrete copious quantities of the original sediment, digesting only a small fraction of the total volume. Among nonselective deposit feeders are various terrestrial and aquatic annelid worms, sea cucumbers (holothurian echinoderms), and a few clam groups. Selective deposit feeders include many scavenging organisms such as certain snails, catfish, and most crabs.

4. **Suspension feeders** strain or filter out of the water microscopic organisms or suspended organic matter. Suspension feeding is carried out by many different groups using a wide assortment of feeding structures. This trophic category includes the baleen whale, which sieves out many thousands of small swimming arthropods using long, fibrous filaments extending from its upper jaw; clams that use their gills to filter suspended organic matter from water passing through the internal mantle cavity; and sponges, which pump water through an elaborate canal system lined with specialized cells for capturing and ingesting small, suspended particles.

5. **Omnivores** are versatile feeders, employing two or often more of the above feeding types. Humans and most other primates are omnivores, as are some bears, some protists and brittle stars.

Distribution of Feeding Types

Clearly, the spatial distribution of organisms in each feeding category is governed largely by the availability of the needed food source. Thus, sedentary suspension feeders prefer habitats where the water is sufficiently agitated to keep

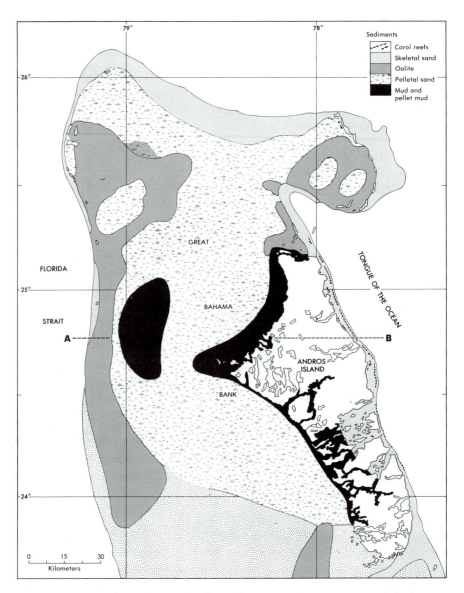

FIG. 4-11 Distribution (above) of major sediment or substrate types and (facing page, top) of bottom-dwelling marine invertebrate communities of the Great Bahama Bank. Note the relatively close coincidence of the distribution of sediment type with the distribution of the bottom communities. At the bottom of the facing page, the cross section (along line A–B of map above) of the shallowly submerged platform that forms the bank indicates the importance of salinity, current velocity, and distance from the deep, open ocean at the bank's margin in determining substrate and, by implication, the bottom communities. The *Acropora* community includes corals, calcareous algae, and foraminiferans; the *Plexaurid* community includes sea fans, sea whips, snails, scattered corals, sponges, and calcareous algae; the *Tivela* community includes a clam, several sea urchins, and marine grasses; the *Strombus* community includes a variety of molluscs and echinoderms; the *Didemnum* community includes a tunicate, green algae, and sponges; the *Cerithidea* community includes a few molluscs, worms, and algae. (After N. D. Newell and others, 1959; E. G. Purdy, 1964; and P. Enos, 1974.)

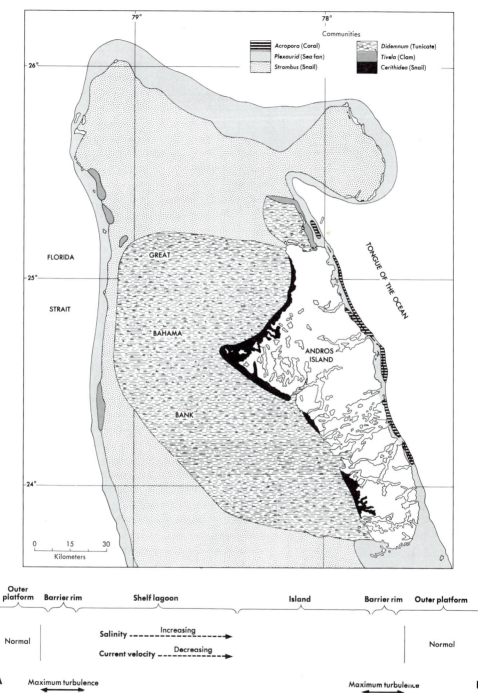

Communities

Acropora (Coral)	Didemnum (Tunicate)
Plexaurid (Sea fan)	Tivela (Clam)
Strombus (Snail)	Cerithidea (Snail)

26°
25°
24°
79°
78°

FLORIDA

STRAIT

GREAT

BAHAMA

BANK

ANDROS ISLAND

TONGUE OF THE OCEAN

0   15   30
Kilometers

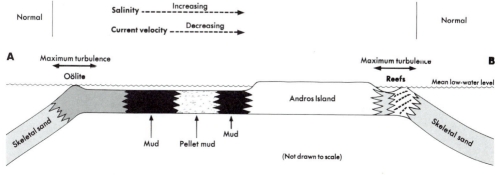

Outer platform	Barrier rim	Shelf lagoon	Island	Barrier rim	Outer platform

Normal

Salinity ---------- Increasing →

Current velocity ---------- Decreasing →

Normal

A

Maximum turbulence ↔

Oölite

Maximum turbulence ↔

Reefs

Mean low-water level

B

Skeletal sand

Mud   Pellet mud   Mud

Andros Island

Skeletal sand

(Not drawn to scale)

organic matter in suspension and continually transported within their feeding range. In quiet water, suspended organic matter settles out on the substrate. Here, there will be many infaunal deposit feeders burrowing through the sediments searching for food.

Carnivore distribution often parallels prey distribution, but peak abundance of higher trophic levels frequently lags in time behind maximum prey abundance. A classic example of this is seen in the population dynamics of the snowshoe hare and its predator, the lynx (Fig. 4-12). This predator-prey link in populations is also very well expressed in temperate freshwater lakes, where seasonal turnover of surface waters provides nutrients for two blooms of phytoplankton production, one in the spring and one in the autumn. The first of these blooms is diatom-rich and is followed by the proliferation of zooplankton that prey upon the diatoms (Fig. 4-13). The link between phytoplankton production and zooplankton increase is equally well demonstrated in marine plankton communities at all latitudes (see polar, temperate, and tropical curves in Fig. 4-14). The offset in growth between producers and consumers in these environments is in part a consequence of the population dynamics of the zooplankton species. (Can you think why?) Similarly, declines in the prey species are usually recorded in population declines of predators. (Also, why?)

The trophic interrelations of different species within an ecosystem can be illustrated as *food chains* or *food webs*. Marine pelagic food chains vary in length according to all the environmental variables discussed earlier in this chapter, but one of the most critical variables in determining the intricacy of pelagic food chains is the seasonal availability of nutrients. Figure 4-15 shows that in areas with high and often variable nutrient influx, such as in upwelling marine waters, food chains are generally very short, with only one or perhaps two levels of carnivorous species. In

FIG. 4-12 Population sizes of the snowshoe hare (solid line) and its predator, the lynx (dashed line), illustrating the close correspondence between population densities of the two species. Data are from the Hudson Bay Company. (From E. P. Odum, 1971.)

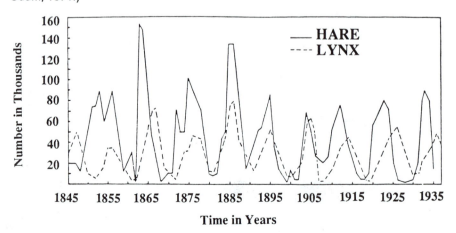

FIG. 4-13 Generalized relationship between phytoplankton (diatoms, shaded), zooplankton (dashed line), sunlight, and nutrients in a temperate to high-latitude lake. Nutrient availability limits plankton growth. (From W. D. Russell-Hunter, 1970.)

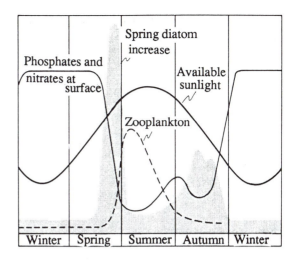

FIG. 4-14 Relationship between seasonal increases in phytoplankton growth (solid line) and zooplankton growth (dashed line) in (A) polar seas, (B) cold-temperate seas, and (C) tropical seas. Note that an increase in zooplankton population follows an increase in phytoplankton population. (From D. Cushing, 1975.)

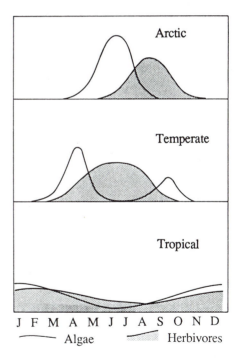

contrast, the midocean, with stable but very low nutrient levels, often has comparatively long food chains of four to six trophic levels. Coastal habitats without upwelling, which receive intermediate nutrient levels, usually have food chains of intermediate length.

A very different sort of ecosystem is the tropical lake, illustrated by the food web diagram in Fig. 4-16. In this example from Gatun Lake in Panama, very small

MARINE PELAGIC FOOD CHAINS

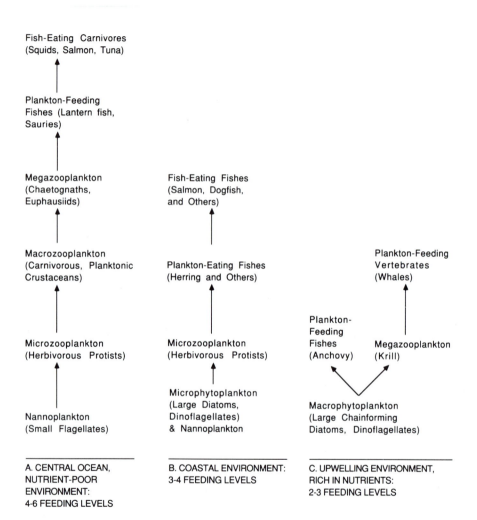

Fish-Eating Carnivores
(Squids, Salmon, Tuna)

Plankton-Feeding
Fishes (Lantern fish,
Sauries)

Megazooplankton
(Chaetognaths,
Euphausiids)

Fish-Eating Fishes
(Salmon, Dogfish,
and Others)

Macrozooplankton
(Carnivorous, Planktonic
Crustaceans)

Plankton-Eating Fishes
(Herring and Others)

Plankton-Feeding
Vertebrates
(Whales)

Microzooplankton
(Herbivorous Protists)

Microzooplankton
(Herbivorous Protists)

Plankton-
Feeding
Fishes
(Anchovy)

Megazooplankton
(Krill)

Nannoplankton
(Small Flagellates)

Microphytoplankton
(Large Diatoms,
Dinoflagellates)
& Nannoplankton

Macrophytoplankton
(Large Chainforming
Diatoms, Dinoflagellates)

A. CENTRAL OCEAN,
NUTRIENT-POOR
ENVIRONMENT:
4-6 FEEDING LEVELS

B. COASTAL ENVIRONMENT:
3-4 FEEDING LEVELS

C. UPWELLING ENVIRONMENT,
RICH IN NUTRIENTS:
2-3 FEEDING LEVELS

FIG. 4-15 Types of pelagic marine food chains. (A) Central oceanic, low-nutrient water mass characterized by long food chains with four to six trophic levels; (B) coastal environments and continental shelves, with intermediate food chain lengths of three to four trophic levels; (C) upwelling coastal marine environments, rich in nutrients, characterized by very short food chains (usually two to three trophic levels). (Data from R. H. Ryther, 1969, and J. Levinton, 1982.)

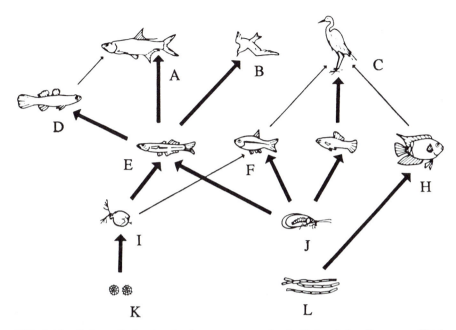

FIG. 4-16 Schematic food web of common species in Gatun Lake, Panama. Thick arrows indicate important links between predator and prey; thin arrows represent minor trophic pathways. Species are: (A) *Tarpon atlanticus,* (B) *Chlidonias niger,* (C) heron and kingfisher species, (D) *Gobiomorus dormitor,* (E) *Melaniris chagresi,* (F) Charanicidae, (G) Poeciliidae, (H) *Cichlasoma maculicauda,* (I) zooplankton, (J) terrestrial insects, (K) nannophytoplankton, (L) filamentous green algae. (From T. M. Zaret and R. T. Paine, 1973, *Science,* v. 182, p. 452. Copyright 1973 by the AAAS.)

phytoplankton (nannophytoplankton) and filamentous green algae provide the photosynthetic base of the ecosystem. Herbivorous consumers include the fish *Cichlasoma,* zooplankton, and terrestrial insects; in turn, predators feeding principally on these herbivores include various fish species. The top-level predators in the ecosystem are a number of bird species (terns, herons, and kingfishers) as well as the predatory fish *Tarpon atlanticus.* In this ecosystem either three or four trophic levels transfer the energy from photosynthesizers to upper-level predators. Unlike the marine habitat, this lacustrine habitat includes faunal components from outside the aqueous medium (terrestrial insects and birds, for example).

Other Biological Interactions

In addition to predator-prey relationships, other ecological interactions between organisms may control their distribution and abundance. *Symbiosis,* which means "living together," refers to these close ecological associations that are normally nonpredatory. Symbiotic relationships are of three types: those that provide mutual benefit to both species (*mutualistic*); those that benefit one species with little or no advantage to the other species (*commensal*); and those that benefit one species but are harmful to the other (*parasitic*).

For example, reef corals in shallow environments are mutualistic with zooxanthellae algae (a kind of dinoflagellate protist). The unicellular zooxanthellae live within the tissues of the coral, where their abundance may be up to half the coral's total biomass! The algae benefit from the supply of carbon dioxide and nitrogen-bearing metabolic wastes generated by the coral. In turn, the host coral benefits from the nutrients produced by the algae and from their photosynthetic oxygen. It also has been amply demonstrated that corals with zooxanthellae can secrete calcareous skeletons up to 10 times faster than corals without zooxanthellae. For this reason, reefs grow far more rapidly when algal symbionts are present within the tissues of the reef-building corals. Corals with zooxanthellae are called *hermatypic corals* or *hermatypes,* whereas those that are not mutualistic with algae are called *ahermatypic corals* or *ahermatypes.* Because of the advantage in higher calcification rate, almost all shallow-water coral reefs are constructed by hermatypes.

In addition to predation and mutualism, *competition* also limits the abundance and distribution of organisms. For sedentary organisms competition for living space on the substrate is particularly vital. Many attached marine organisms such as encrusting bryozoans compete vigorously for space as well as for food; they often preferentially colonize small substrates (such as clam shells) that they can rapidly overgrow, thereby excluding competitors. The interaction between competing bryozoans is well exemplified in the competition between the encrusting genera *Onychella* and *Antropora.* In some experiments *Antropora,* though the faster growing of the two bryozoans, was unable to outcompete *Onychella. Onychella* has a larger feeding organ (lophophore) than *Antropora* and apparently was able to monopolize the food supply in areas in which the two bryozoans co-occurred, hence suppressing the growth of *Antropora,* which was unable to feed freely with its smaller lophophore. This example illustrates well that competition for food and for space are both important for many sedentary organisms. Of course, there are many different types of competition in modern environments. (Can you think of some other examples?)

Chemosynthetic Ecosystems and Symbiosis

All the ecosystems we have considered thus far are based upon photosynthetic sources of energy. There are, however, also marine ecosystems that are fueled principally by *chemosynthetic energy* that flows through food webs involving symbiosis between bacteria and invertebrates (Fig. 4-17). These chemosynthetic ecosystems occur near hydrothermal vents along oceanic ridges or rises where hot, sulfide-rich solutions bubbling out from the earth's crust provide nutrients for chemosynthetic bacteria. Although some populations of bacteria grow in the water column near the vents, most of the bacteria are harbored within invertebrate hosts, such as enormous vestimentiferan worms that grow near the vents. These worms, along with large clams, represent most of the volume of living matter (75 percent) in these prolific

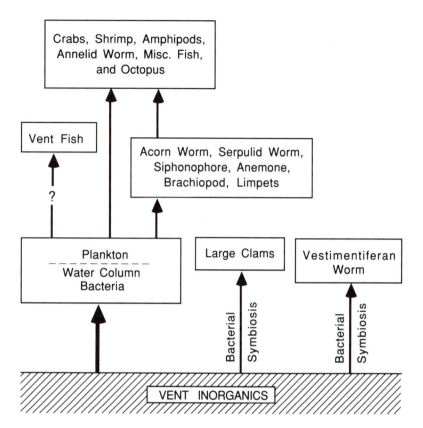

FIG. 4-17 Food web of hydrothermal vent fauna (chemosynthetic food pathway). (Modified from R. R. Hessler and W. M. Smithey, 1983, The Distribution and Community Structure of Megafauna at the Galapagos Rift Hydrothermal Vents, in Rona, P. A., and others, *Hydrothermal Processes at Seafloor Spreading Centers.* New York, Plenum, p. 764.)

communities. The most abundant worms and clams lack the ordinary development of feeding structures and digestive systems, because they obtain their nutrition principally from symbiosis with the active bacterial populations farmed within their tissues. Although details of this chemosynthetic symbiosis are still imperfectly known, this type of community indicates that both chemosynthetic energy and symbiosis may be important controls in some ecosystems.

SUMMARY

Interpretation of the form, or morphology, of an organism involves analysis of the functions of various structures; of architectural or constructional constraints on the design of the organism; and of variations in the surrounding environment. In addition, of course, one must consider the historical or evolutionary limitations upon the taxonomic group being considered.

The distribution and abundance of organisms are controlled by many physical and chemical environmental factors, including temperature, light, availability of carbon dioxide, oxygen, and nutrients, hydraulic energy, and substrate. Each of these environmental factors varies, so that a species may be limited by either the undersupply or oversupply of a given factor. Many aquatic species, for example, are more sensitive to unusually high temperatures than they are to unusually low temperatures.

Biological interactions are also controls on species distribution and abundance. Feeding, or trophic, pathways involve many herbivorous, carnivorous, and omnivorous species; their interactions in the natural environment can be portrayed as simple food chains or as more intricate food webs. Modern communities usually have food chains or webs based on photosynthetic energy from plants or protists, but recently chemosynthesis-based communities have also been discovered near hydrothermal vents along oceanic rises.

In addition to feeding relationships, competition and symbiotic relationships such as commensalism, mutualism, and parasitism may limit the occurrence and abundance of modern organisms. Shallow-water coral reefs, for example, benefit from a mutualistic relationship between corals and symbiotic zooxanthellae algae.

5

TAPHONOMY

I look at the geological record as a history of the world imperfectly kept . . . of this history we possess the last volume alone . . . of this volume, only here and there a short chapter has been preserved . . . of each page, only here and there a few lines. (Charles Darwin. 1859. On the Origin of Species. London: John Murray, 310–11.)

In his great evolutionary work, *On the Origin of Species,* Charles Darwin devoted an entire chapter to analysis of the "imperfection of the geological record." The lengthy discussion of this topic within a treatise on evolution by means of natural selection may surprise many modern readers, but Darwin believed that the lack of abundant fossils intermediate between ancestor and descendant species was the strongest argument that could be presented against his theory of "descent with modification." Darwin interpreted the absence of such transitional fossils as clear evidence of an incomplete fossil record, as the opening quote suggests. Although modern evolutionists now realize that there are evolutionary mechanisms that also explain the sparsity of transitional fossils, Darwin was absolutely correct in stating that much is missing from the fossil record.

Taphonomy (literally, "laws of burial") is the study of all processes affecting the preservation of fossils, from the moment of an organism's death to the discovery of the fossil in a rock outcrop (Fig. 5-1). This field covers a very broad array of studies, including analyses of the inherent preservation potential of different groups of organisms (or different parts of a single organism); measurements of the effects of sedimentation rates upon fossil preservation; and diagenetic investigations of the chemical properties of different skeletal materials. Also included are studies of the rates at which organisms (predators, for example) concentrate or disperse skeletal material that may eventually be included in the fossil record. Finally, taphonomy in-

TAPHONOMY

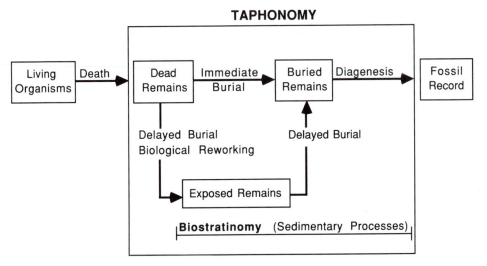

FIG. 5-1 Field of taphonomy as it relates to steps in transformation from living organisms to fossils. (Adapted from A. K. Behrensmeyer and S. M. Kidwell, 1985.)

cludes not only studies that deal with "information loss" between the biosphere and the fossil record but also studies that examine relationships between shell or skeletal material and those living organisms that may use shells of dead organisms as substrates.

PRESERVABILITY OF DIFFERENT ORGANISMS

As we discussed in Chapter 2, organisms that secrete hard parts have a much greater opportunity for fossilization than do soft-bodied organisms. Most fossil assemblages contain only skeletonized remains and therefore include only a tiny sample of the total living community. For example, within a riverbank community of some 10,000 species, it has been estimated that only 10 or 15 are likely to be preserved as fossils. In marine invertebrate communities, such as those near Friday Harbor, Washington, preservation may be much higher; one paleobiologist has suggested that approximately 30 percent of the invertebrates in this rocky intertidal community are potentially preservable as fossils. For a shallow-water, tropical coral reef, perhaps only 50 to 75 species will be fossilized out of a very diverse living biota of 3,000 or more species. Yet, despite these losses, we can usually make important interpretations about the paleoecology of coral-reef environments from the fossils that are preserved.

After an organism dies, oxidation and bacterial decomposition of the organic matrix in which its hard skeleton was secreted, or of the organic tissues that hold the parts together, result in the disarticulation of the individual pieces composing the skeleton. Thus, the many interlocked calcite crystals of a sea urchin become separated, or the two valves of a clam, or the various bones of a vertebrate. Because these disarticulated remains usually come in a range of sizes (refer to Fig. 2-7), some hard parts will be more readily transported by water, as shown in Fig. 5-2. In many environments this separation of hard parts by moving water, *hydraulic sorting,* is an important taphonomic process that can substantially change the proportions of hard parts relative to their original frequencies in the living community. For example, based upon Fig. 5-2, we would expect that streams would transport pig vertebrae far more readily than, say, horse molars because these hard parts would settle out at different flow velocities along the course of the stream, so that even if the pig and the horse originally inhabited the same environment, their skeletal remains, if reworked by moving water, would eventually be deposited in different places.

The skeletal parts of many other terrestrial vertebrates are susceptible to hydraulic sorting in a river channel or along a sloping land surface. Experiments with the skeletons of coyote and sheep indicate which hard parts are easily transported and which are not (Table 5-1). The skull and lower jaw of sheep and coyotes are massive and thus are not easily transported, whereas the disarticulated ribs, vertebrae, and breastbone are much less dense and are moved readily. These experiments give us some insight into interpretation of vertebrate fossil assemblages. If a sample includes bones from group I as well as from groups II and III, we would feel confident in concluding that the assemblage reflects relatively closely the living community. If, on the other hand, the fossil assemblage is com-

FIG. 5-2 Experiments with five different kinds of vertebrate remains yield the equivalent hydraulic grain size for quartz spheres. For example, a horse molar behaves hydraulically as if it were a quartz grain 27 millimeters in diameter, whereas a dermal scute of a crocodile, perhaps one-third the diameter of the horse molar, behaves as if it were a quartz grain only 3 millimeters in diameter. The chief reason for these hydraulic differences is due to the varying densities of the assorted bones and teeth. (From A. K. Behrensmeyer, 1975.)

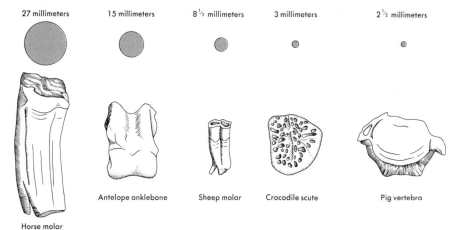

27 millimeters   15 millimeters   8 ½ millimeters   3 millimeters   2 ½ millimeters

Antelope anklebone   Sheep molar   Crocodile scute   Pig vertebra

Horse molar

Table 5-1 Transportability of Sheep and Coyote Bones

GROUP I	GROUP II	GROUP III
Removed Immediately by Saltation or Suspension	Removed Gradually by Traction	Not Removed At All
Ribs	Upper leg bone (femur)	Skull
Vertebrae	Lower leg bone (tibia)	Lower jaw
Breastbone	Upper arm bone (humerus)	
	Wrist/ankle bones	
	Pelvis	
	Lower arm bone (radius)	
Shoulder blade	Lower jaw blade (ramus)	
Finger/toe bones		
Lower arm bone (ulna)		

(After M. R. Voorhies, 1969.)

posed almost completely of Group I bones, then we ought to suspect that the bones have been transported, possibly into a depositional setting far removed from the original habitat.

ENVIRONMENTAL FACTORS

In addition to the presence of hard parts and the physical properties of skeletal material, an organism's environment may also determine its preservation potential. Environments with high sediment accumulation rates typically preserve fossil assemblages that more nearly reflect the living communities than do environments of nondeposition, in which skeletal material is reworked many times or is destroyed before burial (refer again to Fig. 5-1). Table 5-2 illustrates the tremendous range of sedimentation rates known for modern sedimentary environments. Obviously, the marine organisms of deltas stand a better chance of being preserved than those of abyssal plain environments, even though deltaic animals may also be subject to downslope transport.

Hydraulic sorting and transportation of skeletal material away from the original habitat are taphonomic processes that are governed by the environment. Organisms in both terrestrial and marine environments may be subject to transport. Deep-sea cores, for example, often contain turbidites with abundant shallow-water benthic organisms interbedded with fine-grained pelagic sediments containing a deep-sea biota. Studies tracing individual, distinctive turbidite beds suggest that shallow-water skeletal material may in some instances be transported hundreds of kilometers seaward into much deeper water environments.

In other environments the order of abundance of living organisms in the environment may closely parallel the abundance of hardparts in the sediment. In a

Table 5-2 Sedimentation Rates for Selected Modern Depositional Environments

Environment	Range of Sedimentation Rate (meters per million years)	Average Sedimentation Rate (meters per million years)*
Fluvial	65–410,000	86,000
Deltaic	400–450,000	112,000
Coastal wetlands and tidal flats	420–80,000	10,000
Reefs and marine carbonate shoals	35–14,000	2,500
Lakes	150–31,700	5,800
Bays, lagoons, and estuaries	460–14,300	3,600
Bathyal and abyssal environments	0.6–4,500	370
Inland seas	1–2,000	290

*Each of these rates varies tremendously within a given environment; these are unweighted average values. Also, remember that sediments are often reworked or removed by subsequent erosion.
(From D. E. Schindel, 1980.)

Table 5-3 Living and Dead Shelly Invertebrates, Main Channel, Mugu Lagoon, Southern California

Species	A Live	B Dead
Sanguinolaria nuttallii	676	454
Cryptomya californica	204	294
*Dendraster excentricus	42	54
Dipolodonta orbella	15	5
†*Olivella biplicata*	3	16
Chione californiensis	2	6
Spisula dolabriformis	1	2
†*Nassarius fossatus*	1	1
†*Lunatia lewisi*	1	1
†*Polinices reclusianus*	1	1

*Echinoid
†Snails
All the other species are bivalves.
(From J. Warme, 1971.)

classic taphonomic study of a southern California lagoon, it has been demonstrated that the proportions of living clams, sand dollars, and snails very closely resemble accumulations of the dead hard parts of these same organisms in lagoonal sediments (Table 5-3). Thus, in some marine environments, the fossil record of large skeletonized organisms may provide an accurate replica of the living biota.

BIOLOGICAL EFFECTS

Organisms themselves may act as taphonomic agents by redistributing skeletal material by predation, by using hard parts of other organisms to build nests or dwelling structures, or by burrowing. Studies of predation on East African mammals indicate, for example, that predators of gazelles may do great damage to the skeleton, whereas predators of buffaloes usually leave more of the skeleton intact. The use of skeletal materials in forming dwelling structures or nests is also important in taphonomic redistribution of hard parts. Many foraminifera, particularly in the deep sea, construct dwelling tubes or chambers composed of the skeletons of other planktonic organisms. Many of these "agglutinated" foraminifera are highly selective, preferring the hard parts of certain phytoplankton such as coccolithophores, or even using hard parts of single species of other foraminifera. Thus, these agglutinated foraminifera may act to concentrate certain skeletal materials within the sediment.

Terrestrial vertebrates may also collect skeletal materials in and around their nests. In East Africa one of the most prodigious bone-collectors is the porcupine, which, though a vegetarian, gnaws on bones in order to keep its continually growing incisor teeth at the proper length. Porcupines collect large quantities of bone and other hard objects during their nocturnal foraging, which they gnaw upon inside their lair during the day. Large quantities of bones thus accumulate inside the porcupine lairs; one study revealed that over a 12-year period 380 such objects were taken into a lair. More critical from a taphonomic standpoint, however, is that the relative abundance of different bovid species in the lair bones corresponds very closely to living populations in the surrounding Kalahari National Park (Fig. 5-3).

FIG. 5-3 Comparison of census data for living bovids in Kalahari National Park, with frequencies of bone types in the Nossob porcupine lair. (Fig. 7-4, p. 114, from C. K. Brain, in A. R. Behrensmeyer and A. Hill, *Fossils in the Making* (1980); © 1980 by The University of Chicago. All rights reserved.)

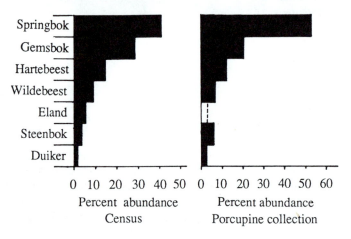

Thus, although the porcupines have concentrated bones, these bone assemblages, if preserved in the fossil record, would provide an accurate reflection of most of the living bovid species in the nearby environment. Other vertebrate bone-collectors, like hyenas, may be more selective, imposing potential biases on the fossil record.

Burrowing by organisms, *bioturbation,* can also redistribute the fossil remains included within sediments as well as alter internal primary structures like cross-stratification or bedding. If there are differences in the proportions of fossil taxa accumulating on the seafloor, layer by layer, these differences may be smoothed out, or obliterated altogether, by later stirring up and mixing of the fossiliferous sediment by burrowers. The smoothing-out process of differences in fossil content in individual layers is called *time-averaging,* because the ongoing reworking of sediments by burrowers—or currents, too, for that matter—tends to average out these variations as the sediments accumulate. Thus, depending on the differential rates of sediment/fossil accumulation and reworking by burrowing, changes in fossil composition from layer to layer through time may still be evident but more gradual and less distinct. Figure 5-4 illustrates the stratigraphic records preserved in two areas that differ in the rates of sedimentary reworking by organisms. In Fig. 5-4(A), no primary sedimentary structures are preserved, because burrowers have reworked the sediments at a rate greater than the rate at which sediment is deposited. In contrast, Fig. 5-4(B) shows an alternation of sedimentation events and periods of intense burrowing, so that some sedimentary structures are preserved. In some sediments, burrowing may be so intense that the sediments are thoroughly homogenized, so that neither burrow outlines nor sedimentary structures can be observed.

FIG. 5-4 (A) Bioturbation going on continuously while sediments are deposited, so that the internal fabric is thoroughly stirred up. (B) Alternating periods of sedimentation without bioturbation followed by periods with active bioturbation. Note sharp erosional break at the end of period of burrowing with overlying laminated, undisturbed sediment. (After A. A. Ekdale, R. G. Bromley, and S. G. Pemberton, 1984.)

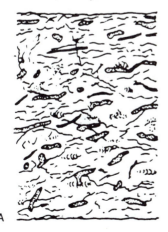
A

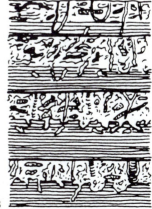
B

In addition to being taphonomic agents, organisms themselves may be directly affected by taphonomic processes. For example, many marine invertebrates require a hard substrate upon which to settle and will frequently use empty shells. Hence, the presence of shell pavements or reworked shelly gravels may provide settlement places for organisms that otherwise would be excluded from the environment. Other organisms, such as hermit crabs, taphonomically recycle empty shells and may transport them to quite different environments because the crabs are dependent upon the availability of empty shells of appropriate size and shape. In turn this availability is, itself, partly a function of taphonomic processes.

DIAGENESIS

A fourth major source of taphonomic bias in the fossil record is *diagenesis,* the process by which loose, wet sediments are transformed into compact, hard rocks. After a sediment is laid down, it is usually buried by successive deposits as the area of sedimentation continues to subside. With increasing burial, the weight of the overlying sediment causes the material below to undergo *compaction* and *consolidation.* Individual sedimentary grains are pushed and crowded together, reducing the initial pore space that formerly existed between grains. In the case of water-laid sediments, the pore fluids are slowly squeezed out as the porosity of the sediment diminishes, sometimes resulting in a volume decrease of 50 percent or more.

As the sediments are compacted, the pore water moves upward through the sediments and may dissolve or precipitate mineral matter along the way. Thus, compaction of sediments and migration of pore fluids initiates the next step in the diagenetic process, *cementation.* Individual sedimentary grains are welded together by minerals precipitated in pore spaces. Cements of silica or calcium carbonate are most common, although other cements do occur. In many sedimentary sequences several generations of cementation are evident, representing diagenetic migration of fluids during different phases of burial or uplift of the sediments.

What happens to the organisms that are buried in sediments undergoing diagenesis? During the first phase, compaction, any soft-bodied remains that survived the effects of erosion, scavenging, and decomposition will be squeezed flat. If the fluids circulating within the sediment during compaction and cementation contain abundant oxygen, the soft-bodied remains will likely be oxidized and destroyed. If, however, there is little or no circulating oxygen, the buried remains may well be preserved as thin carbon films. Preservation of such carbonized remains is common in stagnant or low-oxygen depositional environments, such as those we discussed in Chapter 4.

Buried hard parts composed of opaline silica and calcium carbonate (the minerals aragonite and calcite) are susceptible to *dissolution* during diagenesis. Migrating pore fluids will often dissolve these materials, leaving behind molds in the sediment or sedimentary rock or replacing the original shell material with casts of calcite or silica. Some skeletal compositions are much more susceptible to solution than others. Opaline silica, for example, is a hydrous compound that recrystallizes very rapidly to other silica minerals with elevated temperatures in the subsurface. Similarly, magnesian calcite and aragonite are much less stable mineralogically than calcite. Therefore, an assemblage of potential fossils that includes aragonite (calcareous green algae, corals, some clams and snails), magnesian calcite (calcareous red algae, some foraminifera, and some bryozoans), and calcite (oysters and barnacles) may be differentially preserved, so that only the calcite fossils ultimately remain. In this instance, then, not only are soft-bodied fossils not preserved, but even some of the hard-part secretors fail to survive diagenesis.

AN OLIGOCENE OYSTER COMMUNITY

In order to test specifically just how much and what kind of information is lost during fossilization, paleontologist David Lawrence examined an Oligocene oyster bank in North Carolina and compared the fossils found there with living oyster banks in the same region. The fossil oyster bank of late Oligocene time is lens-shaped and measures 2-1/2 meters high and more than 40 meters long. The oysters initially settled in a 2-meter deep, nearshore channel and built upward and laterally with the passage of time. Sandy sediments accumulated next to the bank and gradually filled the channel, covering most of the oyster deposit. The most abundant fossils in the oyster bank are large oysters, *Crassostrea gigantissima,* which are packed densely together, many of them in their original life position with the left valve encrusting the substrate (usually other oysters or shelly invertebrates). Associated fossils include foraminifera, encrusting bryozoans, spirorbid worms that secrete calcareous tubes, snails, barnacles, and echinoid debris. Besides these body fossils of shelly invertebrates, there are also trace fossils that include borings made by bivalves, bryozoans, sponges, and worms, as well as internal partitions and blisters on the inside of the oysters themselves that record efforts by the oysters to seal off soft-bodied worms that were preying upon them.

Notice that not only do the body fossils tell us which organisms were originally present in the Oligocene oyster community, but the distinctive boring patterns and internal partitions and blisters provide additional evidence of other organisms living in the community. These latter organisms are not fossilized directly because either they were soft-bodied—as in the case of the various worms and sponges—or their aragonite shells were subsequently dissolved—aragonitic bivalves and snails. Such indirect evidence of the original members of the community is *redundant,* in that there is a duplication of information about an organism's initial presence, first by preservation of its hard parts or else by preservation of indirect evidence like traces or borings.

Having established the composition of the fossil oyster community, both by direct evidence of body fossils and by indirect, redundant evidence of soft-bodied and aragonitic forms, Lawrence examined published reports on the faunal composition of modern oyster communities found along the North Carolina coast. The total number of species ranges from around 50 to over 200, depending on the local salinity of the water, with more normal marine saline waters having the higher diversity. Of these species, 80 are quite common and seem to be most characteristic of present-day oyster communities there. These 80 species are listed in Table 5-4, and for each it is indicated whether it is soft-bodied or not and the chemical nature of the hard parts. It is also indicated which species may leave behind redundant information. For example, all five species of sponges secrete microscopic siliceous spicules that reinforce the protoplasmic mass. Not only might these spicules be found as fossils, but three of the species also bore into shells, so that their borings would provide redundant information about their presence. Recognition of such

TABLE 5-4 Fossilization Potential of a Modern Oyster Community

Taxa	Total Species	Soft-bodied	With Preservable Hard Parts				Possible Redundancy
			Ca	Ch	Si	Ph	
Porifera	5	—	—	—	5	—	3
Coelenterata	6	5	1	—	—	—	—
Platyhelminthes	1	1	—	—	—	—	—
Nemertea	2	2	—	—	—	—	—
Bryozoa							
Ectoprocta	7	4	3	—	—	—	—
Annelida							
Polychaeta	13	13	—	—	—	—	4
Mollusca							
Gastropoda	9	—	9	—	—	—	1
Pelecypoda	13	—	13	—	—	—	2
Arthropoda							
Crustacea	19	10	4	5	—	—	5
Arachnida (?)	1	1	—	—	—	—	—
Insecta	1	1	—	—	—	—	—
Chordata							
Tunicata	2	2	—	—	—	—	—
Vertebrata	1	—	—	—	—	1	1
Totals	80	39	30	5	5	1	15
Percentages of total community	100	49	38	6	6	1	19

Among the arthropods, only decapod crabs with relatively well-calcified and/or well-tanned exoskeletons have been included with the organisms with hard parts.
Ca = calcareous
Ch = chitinous
Si = siliceous
Ph = phosphatic
    (From D. R. Lawrence, 1968.)

redundancy is important because the fine-grained, opaline silica of sponge spicules is quite soluble and, consequently, commonly not preserved. This is in fact the case in the Oligocene oyster community, and only the redundancy of sponge borings established their presence. Slightly more than half of the total common species have hard parts; and of these, more than one-third are capable of leaving redundant information.

Next, we can tabulate the kind of calcareous skeletons these living species secreted—whether they were all or mostly calcite, all aragonite, or significant mixtures of the two mineralogies (Table 5-5). This is done to estimate the possible loss of information that would result if the calcareous hard parts were differentially dissolved. Notice that 30 percent of the 80 species secrete either calcite or aragonite in roughly equal proportions (11 species to 13 species), whereas 8 percent secrete a skeleton that is a mixture of the two minerals.

TABLE 5-5 Effect of Aragonite Loss on Preservation of Modern Oyster Community

Taxa	Number of Species	A	C	A + C
Coelenterata	1	—	1	—
Bryozoa	3	—	3	—
Mollusca				
Gastropoda	9	9	—	—
Pelecypoda	13	4	3	6
Arthropoda				
Crustacea	4	—	4	—
Totals	30	13	11	6
Percentage of total community	38	16	14	8

A = completely aragonitic skeletons
C = entirely calcitic skeletons: calcite skeletons with very minor aragonite, as in crassostreids
A + C = appreciable aragonite plus calcite in skeletons
(From D. R. Lawrence, 1968.)

Finally, we can follow the three taphonomic stages that a modern community might pass through during its fossilization history, from the original community with all organisms present, to one where only hard parts and redundancy are preserved, to one where only calcitic remains and redundant information are recorded (Table 5-6). The state of preservability of each of these stages is then compared with what is found in the Oligocene oyster community (column D in Table 5-6). These data strongly indicate that the Oligocene community was quite similar in its composition to a modern oyster community if the latter were to be fossilized. In other words, even though the Oligocene fossil assemblage has fewer fossils, both in kinds and abundance, than the modern community, we can explain this loss of fossils by *predictable* taphonomic processes rather than attribute it to significant differences in original composition of the marine faunas. This example, therefore,

TABLE 5-6 Taphonomic Stages in Preservation of Modern Oyster Community and Comparison with Oligocene Example

	TAPHONOMIC STAGES			OLIGOCENE COMMUNITY
	A →	B →	C	D
Phyla represented	9	7	7	4
Species present	80	45	18	16–18
Percentage of total community preserved	100	56	23	—
Percentage of information through re dundant transmissions—preservation of nonbody parts	0	7	33	~44

└ compare ┘

Column A: original community: all organisms preserved
Column B: all hard parts and all redundant information preserved
Column C: aragonitic, mixed aragonitic-calcitic, chitinous, and siliceous skeletons lost: redundant information preserved
Column D: Oligocene community, for comparison with C
   (After D. R. Lawrence, 1968.)

illustrates the importance of taphonomic analysis in estimating what the original fossil community was like before its subsequent fossilization. As paleoecologists, we want to explain the variations in distribution and abundance of fossil organisms in terms of the original environment. But first we must have a good idea of how much those variations are due to differential preservation and the extent to which they are due to primary environmental causes.

TAPHONOMIC "MEGABIASES" IN THE FOSSIL RECORD

We have discussed a number of taphonomic processes that govern the preservation of different organisms in the fossil record. In addition to the local factors of individual skeletal preservability, depositional rates within the environment, biological activities, and diagenesis, there are larger-scale taphonomic processes that influence the way we view the fossil record of the biosphere as a whole. For instance, global increases in sea level expand the total area of the marine biosphere and thus enhance the volume of marine rocks that can be preserved for that interval of time. In contrast, a drop in global sea level reduces the areal extent of potential marine sediments for that geologic interval.

These global changes in preservational processes have been informally labeled taphonomic "megabiases." Such megabiases are especially evident in compilations of global species diversity through geologic time. An illustration of several types of biases that contribute to estimates of ancient biological diversity can be seen in Fig. 5-5. A number of paleontologists have asserted that global species

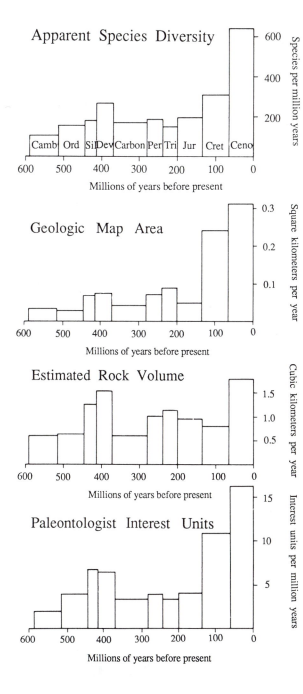

FIG. 5-5 Apparent species diversity for marine environments during Phanerozoic time, in relation to geologic map area, rock volume, and paleontological interest. (From P. Signor, in James W. Valentine, ed., *Phanerozoic Diversity Patterns: Profiles in Macroevolution,* Fig. 4, p. 136. Copyright © 1985 Princeton University Press. Reprinted with permission of Princeton University Press.)

diversity has increased through time, reaching a maximum level in latest Cenozoic time and continuing into today. While it is entirely possible (perhaps even probable) that this conclusion is substantially correct, there are several mega-taphonomic factors that ought to be considered as potential sources of error. For example, Paleozoic maximum species diversity coincides with a stratigraphic interval for which there is also a maximum high point in geologic map area, estimated volume of rock, and "paleontologist interest units" (number of paleontologists working on a given stratigraphic interval); the high volume of rock area and rock volume are, in turn, linked with a mid-Paleozoic high stand of sea level. Thus, an awareness of taphonomic factors is essential not only in interpreting local paleoecological data but also in assessing global compilations of fossil abundances and diversity.

EXCEPTIONAL PALEONTOLOGICAL LOCALITIES

Some of the most dramatic evidence for taphonomic information loss in ancient environments comes from unusual fossil localities that seemingly preserve the full spectrum of living organisms, from soft-bodied to heavily skeletonized. These sites are relatively rare but range in age from Cambrian to Recent. Though few in number, these exceptional localities contribute enormously to our knowledge of evolutionary pathways in poorly skeletonized groups.

Much of what is known about the evolutionary diversification of insects, for example, comes from unusual localities in which organisms have been fossilized in amber. Such sites occur principally in Europe and Central America, and most are of Cenozoic age (though amber itself is known from rocks as old as Carboniferous). Amber, which is the fossilized resin of conifers and a few angiosperms, comes from tree species that extrude large quantities of resin, possibly as a deterrent against pests or predators. Insects, beetles, and other organisms become entrapped in the resin, which is viscous and sticky. In some cases death comes so swiftly to the entrapped organism that feeding or mating is captured in the fossil specimens. Using abundant amber, biologists and paleontologists have been able to reconstruct the evolutionary and biogeographic relationships within groups, such as ants, that are otherwise not preserved in most environments.

Our clearest view of Cambrian soft-bodied life also comes from a series of exceptional fossil localities within the Burgess Shale of British Columbia. In addition to the skeletonized sponges, brachiopods, molluscs, mollusclike hyolithids, and trilobites, numerous soft-bodied or weakly skeletonized organisms include annelid and priapulid worms, arthropods, chordates, and other organisms of uncertain taxonomic affinities. From this unusual fauna three specimens are illustrated in Fig. 5-6 to show the considerable anatomical detail present in fossil specimens of the trilobite *Olenoides* (A), another arthropod (B), and the more bizarre, problematical organism *Wiwaxia* (C).

Simon Conway Morris and his coworkers believe that the excellent preservation within the Burgess Shale results from deposition of the soft-bodied organisms

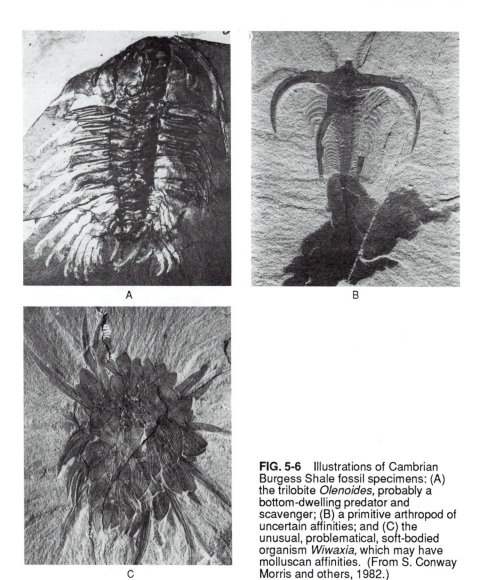

FIG. 5-6 Illustrations of Cambrian Burgess Shale fossil specimens: (A) the trilobite *Olenoides,* probably a bottom-dwelling predator and scavenger; (B) a primitive arthropod of uncertain affinities; and (C) the unusual, problematical, soft-bodied organism *Wiwaxia,* which may have molluscan affinities. (From S. Conway Morris and others, 1982.)

in an anoxic environment, downslope from the original habitat in which the biota lived. Slumping is thought to have carried sediments and organisms out of oxygenated, shallow-water habitats into deeper, anoxic environments where organic matter would not readily be decomposed. The soft-bodied organisms preserved in this manner in the Burgess Shale reflect a transported faunal assemblage that is important from an evolutionary standpoint, for the Burgess soft-bodied organisms represent the Middle Cambrian period, an interval just younger than the Early Cambrian diversification of abundant skeletonized multicellular animals.

SUMMARY

Taphonomy is the study of all processes affecting the preservation of fossils, from the moment of an organism's death to the discovery of the fossil. Included in this study is analysis of the differential preservability of various groups of organisms or even of individual structures (bones, teeth, and so on) within organisms. Mechanical properties of hard parts further determine the stability of the skeletal materials in terms of hydraulic sorting and breakage.

Environmental factors also determine the preservation potential of an organism. Environments with rapid sedimentation rates are much more likely to preserve unreworked skeletal remains than are environments in which slow deposition or erosion is prevalent. Many environments are characterized by extensive downslope movement (for example, turbidites in slope environments), which may strongly affect the quality of preservation of skeletal material.

Organisms can be taphonomic agents when they disperse skeletal material during predation, when they collect skeletal objects as part of nest-building, or when they bioturbate fossiliferous sediment. The diversity of organisms in a community may also depend in a critical way upon taphonomic processes, for many organisms settle on shelly substrates or (as in hermit crabs) inhabit the abandoned shells of dead organisms.

Diagenesis involves compaction, consolidation, cementation, and sometimes also dissolution, all of which may influence fossil preservation. Particularly important as a taphonomic factor is the chemistry of pore fluids during diagenesis, for many skeletal materials are not geochemically stable, particularly when deeply buried beneath overlying sediment.

Taphonomic processes may also affect our view of large-scale problems in paleontology. "Megabiases" exist in the stratigraphic record, so that, for example, fluctuations in sea level may control the volume or area of rock deposited during a given interval, which in turn may govern the total number of species that paleontologists are able to recover from those rocks. The intensity of paleontological study for a given interval may also influence species diversity data on a global scale.

Some of the most striking evidence for the magnitude of taphonomic processes comes not from ordinary fossil sites but from exceptional fossil localities, in which both soft- and hard-bodied fossils are preserved. These exceptional localities are rare but extremely valuable in reconstructing the evolutionary and ecological histories of organisms without well-developed hard parts.

6

PALEOENVIRONMENTAL AND PALEOECOLOGICAL ANALYSIS

Surprisingly detailed interpretations of past environments are possible, and the fossils themselves acquire much added significance whenever they are studied in the full context of their geologic setting. (Norman D. Newell. 1959. Am. Phil. Soc. Proc. 103:277.)

In previous chapters we reviewed some of the relationships among organisms, sediments, and the local depositional environment. But knowledge of these relationships alone will not enable us to reconstruct an *ancient* environment. We also need to develop some insight into just how we go about collecting and examining fossils and rocks so that we can arrive at meaningful conclusions and significant interpretations about ancient life and its environmental setting.

In this chapter, therefore, we will consider some of the assumptions, procedures, viewpoints, and limitations that form the background for paleoecological investigation and interpretation—to ask, in other words, in what sort of general intellectual framework are paleoecological studies pursued? In earlier chapters we discussed paleoecological tactics; here we will discuss paleoecological strategy.

RECONSTRUCTION OF ANCIENT SEDIMENTARY ENVIRONMENTS

Environmental stratigraphy is not merely the cataloging of the characteristics of individual facies but, more significantly, also involves the examination of interrelationships of different facies and the three-dimensional reconstruction of ancient environments. A fourth dimension, time, is also included in stratigraphic interpretations of sedimentary sequences. Hence, environmental stratigraphy is an interpretive

Three-dimensional geometry

Facies definition

FIG. 6-1 Four steps that provide the framework for detailed environmental analysis. See text for discussion.

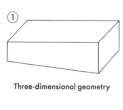

Environmental datum

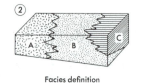

Environmental gradients

discipline through which we can reconstruct environmental variation in both time and space. The resulting paleoenvironment then provides the setting, or context, in which the multitude of animals and plants interacted. Paleoecology is the analysis and interpretation of that interaction.

Usually, the reconstruction of ancient environments requires four separate steps (Fig. 6-1). First, the geometry of the stratigraphic unit has to be defined. We need to know its areal extent, thickness, and the nature of its upper and lower boundaries. Next, we must define and delineate the lithofacies and biofacies in terms of the significant rock and fossil properties of the stratigraphic unit (refer to Chapters 2 and 3). Properties of such lithofacies may include sediment composition, grain size, fabric or grain arrangement, color, bedding, and primary structures like cross-stratification, ripple marks, scour surfaces, and mud cracks. Biofacies characteristics include kinds of fossils—both body fossils and trace fossils—and their abundance, whether the fossils are whole or disarticulated, fresh or worn, reworked or in living position, evenly distributed or found in clumps or clusters, and so on. These lithologic and paleontological variations within a stratigraphic unit record original differences in the depositional environment where the particular sediments and fossils accumulated as well as differences in postmortem taphonomy.

Third, from among the facies we have just defined, we look for one that has a modern analogue or counterpart that is reasonably well understood in terms of the environmental factors responsible for its formation. This facies then becomes an *environmental datum* to which we can refer the other related, but perhaps less well understood, facies. Such a datum might be sun-dried mud cracks, coral reefs, freshwater calcareous algae, oolites, or evaporite salt deposits; any of these would pinpoint somewhere within the total paleoecological complex the existence of certain rather well defined environmental conditions. Rocks and fossils associated directly or indirectly with this datum could then be related ecologically to it, if only by the elimination of other, incompatible, environmental possibilities.

Having established an environmental datum for one facies, we can proceed to the final step in our environmental stratigraphic analysis, which is the prediction of environmental gradients across the strike of the facies. Such gradients include nonmarine to marine; onshore to offshore; shallow shelf to deep-water basin; closed or restricted water circulation to more open, marine circulation; high turbulence to low turbulence; fine-grained to coarse-grained substrate; lowland to upland; more vegetation to less; and so on. We can choose among these various postulated environmental gradients by seeing if the other laterally equivalent facies have attributes consistent with such a gradient.

Returning to the example in Fig. 6-1, facies A might exhibit such features as stromatolites, mud cracks, and other features often found in modern tidal flats (refer to Fig. 3-10). Knowing the origin of this facies, we can predict the kinds of ecological gradients from it into laterally adjacent facies. Thus, we would expect a tidal-flat facies to pass laterally into either a more marine, subtidal facies or a more terrestrial, nonmarine facies, depending, of course, on whether we are moving offshore or onshore from the environmental datum.

We have seen that in many stratigraphic studies examination of the lithologic composition, grain size, and sedimentary structures of a stratigraphic unit permits facies definition and recognition, which in turn contribute to the recognition of ancient environmental gradients. However, besides these traditional methods of facies and environmental analysis, other sources of information, such as geochemical data or trace fossils, can sometimes be used to document environmental gradients. Below we will discuss a few of these additional techniques of gradient analysis.

TRACE FOSSILS

Trace fossils include tracks, trails, and other indirect indicators of the behavior of fossil organisms. Although trace fossils can be difficult to analyze taxonomically (a single organism may make different tracks at different times or, conversely, different animals may produce similar tracks and trails), we can usually interpret the behavior that such a fossil represents: dwelling, feeding, crawling, resting, and so on (see Fig. 6-2). Trace fossils have been used widely to refine paleoenvironmental reconstructions, particularly for marine sedimentary rocks. They occur in a very wide spectrum of sedimentary facies and, unlike body fossils, cannot generally be physically reworked or transported out of the original depositional environment without being destroyed. Also, tracks and trails are often enhanced through diagenesis, becoming more distinct after lithification than in the original soft sediment, unlike body fossils, which may be dissolved or recrystallized.

Traces produced by modern marine organisms are zoned according to the onshore-offshore energy gradients in the environments they inhabit (Fig. 6-3). For instance, marine organisms in the high-energy, sandy habitats along shorelines dwell in vertical burrows that protect them from the highly turbulent waters above the substrate. An example of this assemblage of vertical trace fossils is illustrated in the *Skolithos* assemblage in Fig. 6-3; the *Skolithos* association has been identified as an environmental datum for shallow, high-energy, nearshore facies in numerous paleoenvironmental studies. The deeper, quieter waters of the outer continental

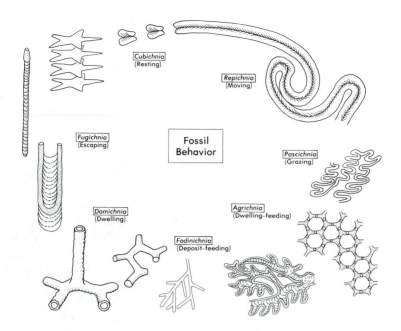

FIG. 6-2 Categories of trace fossils according to type of behavior. Formal terms for each type are given with their informal description in parentheses. Generic names associated with each type, from upper right and continuing clockwise, are: *Cruziana, Cosmorhaphe, Paleodictyon, Phycosiphon, Chondrites, Thalassinoides, Ophiomorpha, Diplocraterion, Gastrochaenolites, Asteriacites,* and *Rusophycus*. (From A. A. Ekdale, R. G. Bromley, and S. G. Pemberton, 1984, p. 24.)

shelf, slope, and abyss allow animals to feed and move about by browsing or grazing along the sediment surface, so that in these environments complex, horizontal burrows and traces are predominant (see, for example, the *Cruziana, Zoophycos,* and *Nereites* assemblages in Fig. 6-3). This onshore-offshore trend in trace fossil assemblages, which reflects varying energy levels in marine environments, can sometimes be used to recognize environmental gradients in stratigraphic sections. However, because individual trace fossils occasionally present exceptions to the overall onshore-offshore trend, it is important to consider whole assemblages rather than isolated specimens when using trace fossils as environmental indicators. Trace-fossil associations are most valuable when used in conjunction with lithologic or geochemical data to define environmental gradients.

GEOCHEMICAL EVIDENCE

Data from isotopes, major elements, and trace elements of fossils and sedimentary rocks have become increasingly important in reconstruction of ancient environmental gradients. These geochemical lines of evidence may be used in paleogeographic reconstruction for a given geologic interval or, alternatively, in analysis of climatic variation through time as recorded in a series of vertical

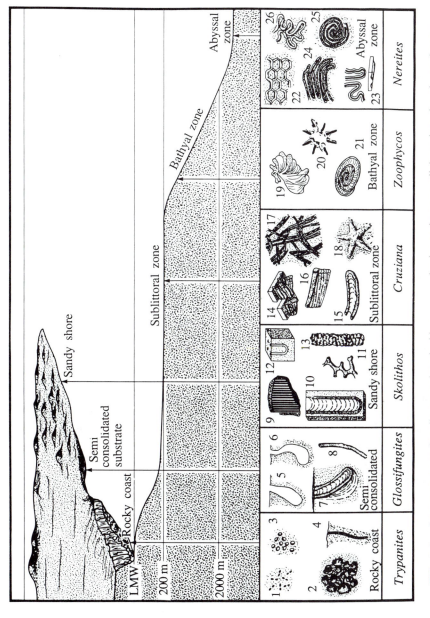

FIG. 6-3 Common trace fossils associated with a typical onshore-offshore transect, illustrating the prevalence of vertical traces (mainly tubes) nearshore and the increasing dominance of more intricate, horizontal traces offshore into the abyssal zone. (From A. A. Ekdale, R. G. Bromley, and S. G. Pemberton, 1984.)

101

stratigraphic sections. With the aid of geochemical techniques, for example, the intricate series of glacial advances and retreats of the late Pleistocene epoch can be correlated with the ages of marine sediments worldwide (see Chapter 7), a connection that would have been very difficult to establish if based only on lithologic or paleontological data. Geochemical data are now used routinely in analysis of ancient marine, lacustrine, and terrestrial sediments; advances in this field are occurring very rapidly. Among the many geochemical methods now being used in environmental analysis, isotopic methods are some of the most frequently applied in environmental gradient analysis.

Isotopic Evidence

Information from *isotopes* of skeletal grains is widely used in characterizing ancient environments. Isotopes are different forms of the same element, containing identical numbers of protons but different numbers of neutrons in the nucleus; hence, the various isotopes of an element have the same atomic number but contrasting atomic masses. You may be familiar with the geologic use of unstable radioactive isotopes of carbon or uranium in dating a wide variety of rocks. In contrast, for environmental analysis stable isotopes are more generally useful than unstable radioactive isotopes. This is because, unless the fossils of rocks are altered through diagenesis, the stable isotope "signature" of a skeletal grain will not spontaneously alter through time; in the absence of diagenetic alteration, this signature will record original conditions within the organism or depositional environment.

The element oxygen—which is, of course, a constituent of calcium carbonate ($CaCO_3$)—has several different stable isotopes. These isotopes, designated ^{16}O, ^{17}O, and ^{18}O, have relative abundances in the modern ocean of 99.76, 0.04, and 0.20 percent, respectively. We know, however, that the ratios of different oxygen isotopes vary with environment and with time according to a number of environmental and climatic factors. Three factors seem to be quantitatively most significant in accounting for the environmental variation in oxygen isotopes: the volume of glacial ice in the oceans, the temperature of the seawater, and the salinity of the seawater. Recognition of these three factors allows us to use oxygen isotopes to interpret those ancient environmental and climatic variations that had an influence on oceanic water masses.

In the Cenozoic stratigraphic record a large fraction of the variation in oxygen isotopes relates to the waxing and waning of continental ice sheets. As water evaporates from the ocean and is precipitated in polar ice, the heaviest isotope, ^{18}O, tends to remain in seawater. Consequently, during glacial episodes marine seawater is enriched in ^{18}O relative to the lighter counterpart, ^{16}O. The temporal variation in these isotope ratios is remarkably clear in Cenozoic deep-sea cores, as shown in Fig. 6-4; glacial and interglacial intervals can be readily identified, respectively, by major variations of heavy and light isotopes in the stratigraphic record. Use of this technique can therefore help to resolve paleoclimatic environmental gradients in cores and outcrops.

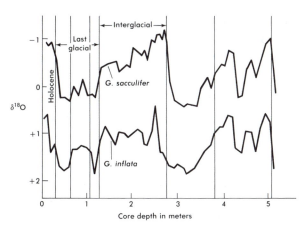

FIG. 6-4 Variation of oxygen isotopes of two planktonic foraminifera as a function of depth in a Holocene to late Pleistocene core from the southern Indian Ocean. The oldest sediments represented by this graph are approximately 260,000 years old. (From J. Kennett, 1982; after J. C. Duplessy, 1978.)

Another source of variation in oxygen isotope signatures is the temperature of the surrounding water. This type of isotopic variation is well demonstrated in the skeletal carbonate or silica of modern organisms that dwell in seasonally variable environments. For example, skeletal growth in the giant Indo-West Pacific clam, *Tridacna maxima*, shows seasonal changes in ^{18}O composition that correlate with annual cycles (Fig. 6-5); note the oscillation between heavy (cool) isotopic layers and light (warm) isotopic layers as the shell grew. Note also that for this animal the oxygen isotopes reveal a distinct decrease in growth rate that accompanies sexual maturity at about 10 years. For this organism and many others, oxygen isotope analysis of skeletal material reveals valuable paleoecological information.

Evaporation rates within a sedimentary basin may also contribute to the oxygen isotope signatures of sediments, although this factor is usually less impor-

FIG. 6-5 Oxygen isotopes sampled from early to late growth phases in the shell of the giant clam, *Tridacna maxima*. Circled numbers indicate yearly increments on shell; note decrease in growth rate at approximately 10 years, probably related to the onset of sexual maturity. Seasonal changes in $^{18}O/^{16}O$ relationships of skeletal carbonate are particularly well expressed in years 1 to 9. (From D. S. Jones, D. F. Williams, and C. S. Romanek, 1986, *Science,* v. 231, p. 46. Copyright 1986 by the AAAS.)

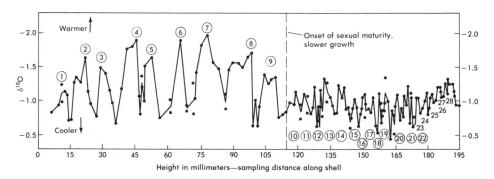

tant than the two we discussed above. As in the glacial situation, high rates of evaporation cause the remaining seawater to be enriched in the heaviest isotope, ^{18}O; hence, highly saline waters have heavy isotopic signatures (high proportion of ^{18}O to ^{16}O). For example, the modern Mediterranean Sea has a well-known salinity gradient, from normal marine salinities of 36.5 parts per thousand in the eastern North Atlantic Ocean and just inside the Straits of Gibraltar, to elevated salinities of more than 38.5 parts per thousand in the eastern Mediterranean and Black seas (Fig. 6-6). Vertical salinity profiles at three sites in the Mediterranean clearly show a corresponding change in oxygen isotope values in seawater, from the lighter values of normal marine waters of the western Mediterranean, to the heavier values of the hypersaline eastern Mediterranean; this confirms that oxygen isotope ratios of modern seawater accurately reflect regional salinity trends. Isotopic results from ancient inland seas or coastal areas may also allow resolution of salinity gradients in the stratigraphic record, because whereas salinity may not be directly inferred from fossils or sediments, systematic variations in salinity may be revealed by their isotopic composition.

Oxygen isotopes have also proven to be powerful tools in unraveling the diagenetic histories of sedimentary rocks. Because oxygen isotopes are sensitive to

FIG. 6-6 (A) Map of salinity (S‰; parts per thousand) of seawater in the modern Mediterranean Sea. Note the increase in salinity from the Straits of Gibraltar eastward to the Black Sea. (B) Salinity profiles of seawater versus water depth at three stations (A, B, C) ranging from normal marine salinity (A) to hypersaline (C). Note that the hypersaline station, C, has elevated ^{18}O values. (From C. Vergnaud-Grazzini, 1985; reprinted by permission of Springer-Verlag.)

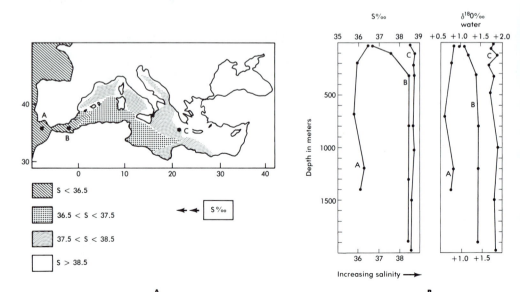

thermal changes, they often reflect postdepositional processes that influence temperature rather than primary geochemical signals from the depositional environment. For this reason we cannot uncritically apply oxygen isotope data to paleoenvironmental problems. Before we can use this type of data, we must consider the possibility of secondary diagenetic alteration; instead of measuring variations in temperature in the original environment, we might be measuring the later burial temperature of the fossils or rocks.

Carbon Isotopes

The stable isotopes of carbon, ^{12}C and ^{13}C, occur in varying proportions within calcium carbonate skeletons and in different kinds of nonmarine and marine organic matter. The ratio of ^{13}C to ^{12}C can be very useful in determining the origin of organic matter in marine sedimentary rocks, because various types of organic matter have distinctly different carbon isotope content. It is often possible, for example, to discriminate between marine and nonmarine plant matter by using carbon isotopes from the organic residues in a sedimentary rock (Fig. 6-7). Once again, this technique cannot be applied uncritically, however, because of overlapping carbon isotope ranges in several groups and also because there are exceptions known for many of the carbon isotope ranges plotted in Fig. 6-7.

Carbon isotopes have also been used recently to answer global oceanographic questions. For example, how has marine primary productivity varied through geologic time? One can use the carbon isotope signatures of marine skeletal grains as an indirect answer to this question because the higher the biological production of photosynthesizers in the water column, the greater the fractionation of carbon

FIG. 6-7 Variations in carbon isotope ratios ($^{13}C/^{12}C$) in natural materials from different environments. Note that land plants, fossil wood, and coal all have about the same ratio, supporting other evidence that coal is formed from land plants. Petroleum, on the other hand, apparently derives from only the lipid portion, or fats and waxes, of marine and nonmarine plants. (From R. M. Garrels and F. T. Mackenzie, 1971; and Anderson and Arthur, 1983.)

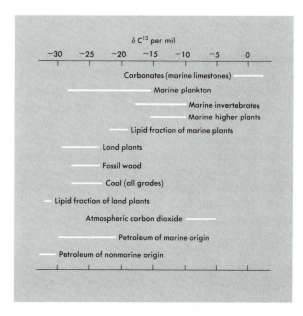

isotopes. The sedimentary signal that is preserved from the accumulated organic carbon depends on numerous factors, including the rate of preservation of the organic matter in the sediment and the diagenetic history of the preserved sediment. However, in some cases, actual changes in global aquatic productivity have been inferred from isotopic variations. For example, Fig. 6-8 illustrates a general decline in ^{13}C in rocks above the Cretaceous-Tertiary boundary at a number of widely distant stratigraphic sections; this decrease in ^{13}C probably signals a decline in global marine productivity following the Cretaceous mass extinction.

Sulfur Isotopes

Sulfur isotopes are also useful in sedimentologic analysis, particularly for sediments rich in pyrite (iron sulfide). Four stable isotopes of sulfur occur in nature: ^{32}S, 95.02 percent; ^{33}S, 0.75 percent; ^{34}S, 4.21 percent; and ^{36}S, 0.02 percent. Isotopic ratios of sulfur are expressed in terms of the relative abundances of ^{34}S and ^{32}S, which vary in sediment principally because of the biological activity of anaerobic bacteria, such as *Desulfovibrio desulfuricans*. These bacteria, which derive energy from the reduction of sulfate, preferentially use the lightest isotope, ^{32}S, so that sediment in which these bacteria thrive may record a high degree of fractionation of sulfur isotopes. Sulfur isotopes can thus be used as indicators of the influence of sulfur-reducing bacteria in sedimentary or diagenetic environments where oxygen-free conditions existed.

Application of sulfur isotope data to sedimentologic problems also requires a correction for the age of the sediments being considered, because the global ratio of ^{34}S to ^{32}S has varied significantly through Phanerozoic time. Ordinarily this correction is relatively simple and is based on established curves for the variation in the global sulfur ratio.

OCEANOGRAPHIC AND CLIMATIC MODELING

Once environmental gradients are recognized in local stratigraphic studies, they can be compared with regional or global trends. For example, the onshore-offshore trend in Fig. 6-1 could be placed in the context of other known shorelines of comparable age to gain a broader paleogeographic perspective. Similarly, deepening-upward or shallowing-upward stratigraphic sequences within a single basin, such as the Mediterranean, may be congruent with, or contrary to, global sea-level trends for that same geologic interval. Often, global patterns of sea-level rise and fall can be determined by observing time-equivalent deepening or shallowing of stratigraphic sequences in widely separated areas. For example, stratigraphers have long speculated that the Late Permian to Early Triassic was an interval of very low global sea level, because at most sections worldwide this interval is marked by a gap in sedimentation (see, for example, the curve in Fig. 3-2). Such global models depend on careful stratigraphic analysis of individual sections, which then should be

Carbon Isotope Profiles Across the Cretaceous–Tertiary Boundary

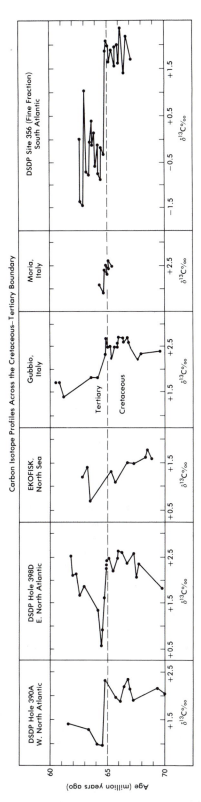

FIG. 6-8 Variation in carbon isotope ratios near the Cretaceous–Tertiary boundary; data from whole-rock analysis of pelagic limestones at three Deep-Sea Drilling Project sites, two outcrop localities in Italy, and a well in the North Sea. The sediment analyzed in DSDP site 356 consists primarily of calcareous nannofossils. (From P. A. Scholle and M. A. Arthur, 1980, reprinted by permission of American Association of Petroleum Geologists.)

placed in a regional or global context. In Chapter 7 we will discuss several case studies in which this unified approach has been used.

PALEOECOLOGICAL ANALYSIS

The reconstruction of ancient ecosystems requires a prior understanding of the three- (or four-) dimensional array of paleoenvironments preserved in a given suite of sedimentary rocks. The challenge of paleoecological analysis is to integrate this paleoenvironmental context with the pattern of faunal or floral associations preserved in the rocks. Furthermore, the goal of paleoecology is not only to connect fossils with facies but also to examine the interrelationships of different fossil biotas in space and time.

Diversity Profiles

A first step in paleoecological analysis is simple taxonomic characterization of fossils contained in a stratigraphic unit or section, followed by tallying of numbers of species within each stratigraphic horizon and within each major taxonomic group. From these compilations, diversity analyses can be made. These analyses may involve only lists of the distributions of taxa, or, alternatively, they may also include quantitative measures of the frequencies of different taxa. For example, how evenly distributed are the various species? Are all species equally abundant, or are there a few dominant forms and a host of rare taxa? This diversity and frequency analysis contributes much information about an assemblage, over and above a mere species list; two assemblages may have identical taxonomic lists but entirely different proportions of included species (Fig. 6-9).

Trophic and Substrate Analysis

Ecological classification of fossil assemblages may be done in several ways; two standard approaches are trophic and substrate analyses. We discussed in Chapter 4 the spectrum of trophic (feeding) and substrate/locomotion relationships among modern organisms. Here we will illustrate how these various ecological categories can be used to classify and compare various fossil assemblages.

Trophic analysis involves defining feeding relationships for each taxon in the biota (see summary of these feeding categories in Chapter 4), then compiling and analyzing the frequencies of the different trophic groups (suspension feeders, deposit feeders, predators, and so on). Analysis may be carried out in two ways: according to either the number of individual fossils in each trophic group or to the number of species represented in each group. Sometimes it is helpful to compile the data both ways for comparative purposes. The relative frequencies of different trophic groups can then be portrayed graphically, on a ternary plot or other diagram, so that different assemblages may be compared visually. Figure 6-10(A) illustrates various benthic marine communities and the differing proportions of feeding types in each.

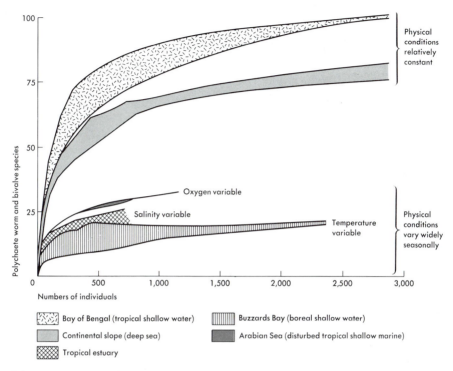

FIG. 6-9 Diversity plots for five different benthic marine environments, showing the influence of varying physical conditions on the numbers of species of marine worms and clams. The shape of each of the curves indicates that as more and more individual animals are observed in an environment, fewer and fewer new species are encountered. In the Bay of Bengal and along the deep-sea continental slope, physical conditions are relatively constant; here the benthic communities are "biologically accommodated." The other three environments experience wide seasonal fluctuations in oxygen, salinity, or temperature; here the communities are "physically controlled" and have much lower diversity. (After H. Sanders, 1968.)

In a similar way *substrate analysis* uses substrate and locomotor groups within an assemblage as a means of classification. As with trophic analysis, either numbers of individuals or numbers of taxa within each group may be compiled. The resulting frequencies may then be plotted on a ternary diagram; fields can be defined for sessile infaunal, sessile epifaunal, and mobile groups, or for other combinations that are most appropriate to the study (see Fig. 6-10(B)). The fields for samples on the trophic and substrate diagrams can then be compared; they often indicate distinct faunal or floral associations that differ from others in both feeding and locomotion.

We have indicated that in trophic and substrate analysis either individuals or species can be counted. Recently, it has also been shown that for some modern faunal associations correspondence in relative proportions between the original living faunas and the dead shelly faunas in the underlying sediment is highest if one

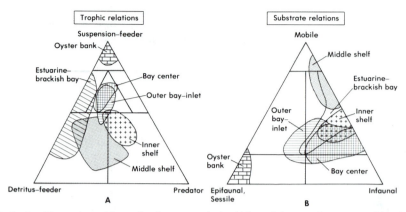

FIG. 6-10 Plots of trophic and substrate relationships of Cenozoic communities in several marine environments. Note that although the spatial location of the fields for associations varies, each association type (for example, oyster bank) remains fairly distinct. (From R. W. Scott, 1978.)

measures *biomass* (amount of living material) of each species in the fossil accumulation, rather than counting only numbers of specimens. Biomass also offers a more precise way of examining energy flow in fossil assemblages than do counts of individuals or species. (Why is this so?) This method therefore seems to have considerable potential for more precise reconstruction of ancient communities.

There are many different ways of quantitatively analyzing for benthic associations or paleocommunities in these three modes (that is, number of individuals, number of taxa, or biomass proportions). Most paleoecological studies now include multivariate statistical techniques to discriminate paleocommunities or associations rather than relying solely on the semiquantitative approaches of ternary plots. These more advanced, multivariate quantitative approaches usually also emphasize trophic and substrate groupings.

REGIONAL AND GLOBAL PALEOECOLOGICAL ANALYSIS

The paleoecological analysis of stratigraphic sections represents more than just a descriptive exercise for determining local changes in ancient ecosystems. In fact, a number of broader applications can be made from paleoecological studies. For example, the diversity of associations in one area can be compared with associations of comparable age in other areas to discern possible ecological gradients on a regional or basinal scale or to address more global biogeographic questions. Another approach in using paleoecological data is to examine the vertical changes in various faunal or floral associations for evidence of community replacement, an ecological process operating on time scales of 10^5 to 10^7 years (see Chapter 1). On a global scale, studies of mass extinctions also depend on knowledge of the paleoecology of individual stratigraphic sections at key localities around the world. Thus, local paleoecological studies can contribute greatly to large-scale paleontological questions, much in the same way that facies analysis of individual sections and sequences can yield answers to questions about global sea level and climate.

SUMMARY

The three-dimensional reconstruction of ancient environments is one of the principal goals of the science of environmental stratigraphy. The steps involved in paleoenvironmental reconstruction are fourfold, beginning with delineation of the extent, geometry, and boundaries of the rock unit. The second phase involves the characterization and definition of individual rock facies, based primarily upon lithology and sedimentary structures, as well as of biofacies, based upon the fossil content and taphonomic characteristics of the stratigraphic unit. Next, the individual facies are examined for an environmental datum—a lithofacies or biofacies that reflects a unique and distinctive depositional environment (for example, a tidal-flat facies). Finally, the surrounding facies are compared with the environmental datum to reconstruct environmental gradients. Recognition of environmental gradients can be strengthened by using supplemental lines of evidence, including trace-fossil assemblages and geochemical data (particularly the light, stable isotopes of oxygen, carbon, and sulfur).

Paleoecological analysis seeks to reconstruct ancient ecosystems, including both organism-sediment and organism-organism interactions. Paleoecological reconstruction of paleocommunities or associations begins with the characterization of faunal and floral species and the analysis of the frequency distribution of included fossil species. Following diversity analysis, a paleoecologist would examine the feeding and locomotor characteristics of the fossil assemblage to quantify the proportions of suspension feeders, predators, and so on. This tally of the feeding and locomotor aspects of fossil assemblages should allow the classification of different ecological associations within the array of fossil assemblages within a particular stratigraphic unit.

Both paleoenvironmental and paleoecological analysis can be used to resolve regional and global problems of climate, sea level, and extinction, using individual stratigraphic sections from around the world as case studies. In the next chapter we will look at several case studies from the paleoenvironmental and paleoecological literature.

7

ENVIRONMENTAL SYNTHESIS

Our task, then, is to identify the remains that lived together, reconstruct . . . the community structure . . . and infer its ecological and evolutionary significance. (James W. Valentine. 1973. Evolutionary Paleoecology of the Marine Biosphere. *Englewood Cliffs, N.J.: Prentice-Hall, 308.)*

Having discussed the interactions of organisms, sediments, and environments, how they are displayed (or not displayed) in the stratigraphic and fossil record, and some of the assumptions and methods of environmental analysis, we now turn to several specific examples to indicate how paleoecologists read out ancient environments and what their general significance might be for historical geology. The examples are chosen from widely different parts of the stratigraphic record: marine and terrestrial rocks, carbonates and clastics, macrofossils and microfossils, invertebrates and vertebrates, Paleozoic, Mesozoic, and Cenozoic times.

The first example comes from Devonian limestones that were deposited at the edge of a transgressing sea in central New York. Based upon our knowledge of modern carbonate environments, the physical characteristics of these limestones indicate deposition in tidal-flat and shallow subtidal environments, with varying degrees of water energy and circulation. The biofacies associated with these environments can then be interpreted in terms of their major ecological controls. This example from the Devonian period indicates the usefulness of working out the environmental stratigraphy before interpreting the paleoecology of the fossils.

Our second example is from the Late Jurassic terrestrial rocks of western North America. Here we find a semiarid environment with diverse assemblages of herbivorous and carnivorous dinosaurs as well as a few scattered remains of early mammals. Mountain-building along the Pacific edge of the continent created a broad belt of riverine, lacustrine, and marshy environments to the east—from Montana and the Dakotas in the north to Arizona and New Mexico in the south—where erosional debris from the mountains accumulated as the Morrison Formation. Great herds of dinosaurs roamed across this landscape, following seasonal changes in rainfall and vegetation, eventually leaving behind one of the richest deposits of vertebrate fossils found anywhere in the world. So abundant are these reptilian remains that we are able to reconstruct fairly completely the terrestrial communities of this dinosaurian heyday, obtaining insights into the taphonomy, population structure, and habitat preference of these fascinating creatures.

Our third example, from Miocene marine sediments of California, provides a very different paleoecological approach from the previous two examples. Here we use the general ecology of planktonic microfossils to estimate the oceanic environments of the eastern Pacific Ocean some 5 to 20 million years ago. We will do this not only by referring to the marine habitats preferred by the modern equivalent microfossils but also by using the isotopic composition of their shells, or tests, to infer changing character of the water masses in which they lived, changes that are in turn related to global cooling during the Miocene. We will thus see how the present is, indeed, a key to the past.

Our final example, from the Pleistocene deep-sea sediments of the North Atlantic, continues the logic of the previous example in a more detailed, quantitative way. Here we use the ecology of *living* species of microfossils to read out the marine conditions that existed tens to a few hundreds of thousands of years earlier. Initially, this can be done qualitatively: Assemblages of extant, warm- and cold-water species in cores indicate past warm and cold intervals during Pleistocene time, intervals that can be measured *absolutely* (in years) with radioactive isotopes. It is further possible to determine, *quantitatively,* the temperature and salinity of the sea surface where these microfossils lived, both from stable isotopes of their tests and from absolute temperature and salinity preferences of particular living species. We can then measure the rate and degree of ocean temperature variation over a long enough period of time to determine the cyclicity of global climatic change that these ocean temperatures record. As such details of past global climate are clarified, we may draw conclusions about future climate. Thus, as the present is a key to the past, the past in turn becomes a guide to the future.

EARLY DEVONIAN SEA OF NEW YORK

Across central New York and down along the Hudson River valley, Early Devonian marine limestones and shales record a regional transgression of a shallow sea, northward and westward, through West Virginia, western Maryland, central Pennsylvania, and into central New York. These rocks form the Helderberg Group, which comprise a sequence of limestone and shale formations, with each formation containing distinctive fossil assemblages and rock types (Fig. 7-1). Because each Helderberg formation could be differentiated from another, particularly on the basis

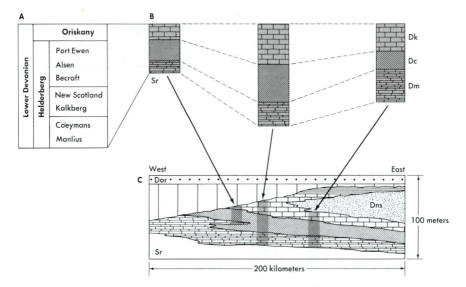

FIG. 7-1 (A) The Helderberg Group of marine limestones and shales in central New York. (B) At one time, each formation was thought to be the same age throughout the region, owing to the distinctive fossils of each formation. (C) Later detailed field work showed that the formations interfingered with one another and recorded a series of sedimentary facies, migrating laterally and building up vertically over time. The distinctive fossils of each facies reflect, therefore, different marine environments rather than significantly different geologic ages. Sr denotes the Rondout Formation of the Late Silurian period; Dm, Dc, Dk, and Dns are the Manlius, Coeymans, Kalkberg, and New Scotland formations of the Early Devonian period; Dor is the Oriskany Sandstone, also Early Devonian, that lies uncomformably on the Helderberg Group, owing to pre-Oriskany/post-Helderberg erosion. (After L. F. Laporte, 1969.)

of its fossil content, early geologists interpreted this to mean that each of the formations was deposited uniformly across the whole area. Differences in their respective fossils were viewed as the simple result of evolution over the time during which the rocks were deposited.

Stratigraphy and Facies

However, later, careful stratigraphy by L. V. Rickard demonstrated that these formations are better interpreted as the accumulated record of a series of laterally migrating, shallow-water environments accompanying regional transgression. Hence, the *vertical* Helderberg stratigraphy represents the *lateral* biofacies and lithofacies of this shallow sea of Early Devonian time (refer to Fig. 7-1, and recall the discussion of Walther's law in Chapter 3).

Given this three-dimensional geometry, we can examine the middle portion of the Helderberg Group across the west-east length of outcrop to observe the lateral variations in the lithology, paleontology, and primary structures of these different facies to see if we can reconstruct the original depositional environments. We might think of this as if we were rowing a boat across the ancient Helderberg sea, taking

TABLE 7-1   Lateral Facies Variations in the Helderberg Group

Stratigraphic Units	WEST — Manlius	Coeymans	Kalkberg	EAST — New Scotland
Lithology	Pellets and intraclasts	Skeletal debris	Carbonate mud	Terrigenous mud
	Early dolomite	Sparite		
Paleontology	Algal structures and calcareous algae			Sponges
	Stromatoporoids	Tabulate corals		
	Rugose corals		Bryozoans	
		Brachiopods		
	Snails			
	Clams			
	Tentaculitids			
		Ostracods		
			Trilobites	
		Pelmatozoans		
Structures	Mud cracks			
	Erosion surfaces			
		Cross-stratification		
	Vertical burrows			
			Horizontal burrows	
Environment	Tidal flat-lagoon; poor circulation. Highly variable environment.	High and low energy subtidal; good circulation. Stable environment except for varying water agitation.	Open, shallow shelf; low energy. Highly stable environment with good circulation. Low terrigenous influx.	Open, shallow shelf; low energy. Variations caused by periodic terrigenous influx.

(After L. F. Laporte, 1969.)

bottom samples of the marine life and sediments on the seafloor and then attempting to explain what environmental factors were important in controlling the distribution and abundance of the biotas and sediments. Table 7-1 and Figs. 7-2 and 7-3 summarize the results of this lateral facies analysis.

Paleoecology

How then are we to interpret these rocks and fossils? First, the presence of mud cracks and local erosion surfaces (scour-and-fill structures) with associated intraclasts indicates intermittent subaerial exposure of marine sediments that make up large portions of the Manlius Formation. We know that these are marine sediments,

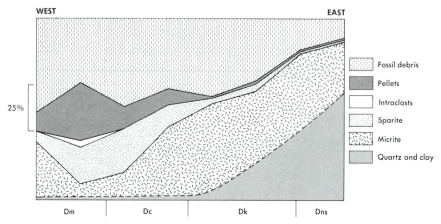

FIG. 7-2 Variation in the composition of the lateral equivalents of the Manlius, Coeymans, Kalkberg, and New Scotland formations, which are limestones and calcareous shales. Pellets include both fecal pellets and small erosional carbonate clasts; intraclasts are larger erosional clasts; sparite is secondarily precipitated calcite within interstices of original grains; micrite is fine-grained, recrystallized carbonate mud; clastic components include quartz silt and clays. (After L. F. Laporte, 1969.)

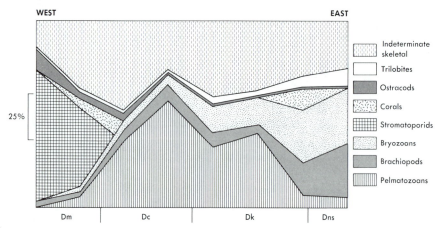

FIG. 7-3 Variations in composition of fossil debris shown in Fig. 7-2. Some debris is so fine-grained that it is simply labeled indeterminate skeletal. Pelmatozoans include both crinoids and cystoids. Note the systematic variation in fossil composition from the Manlius Formation through its lateral equivalents. (After L. F. Laporte, 1969.)

owing to the scattered remains of marine organisms, such as brachiopods, bryozoans, and corals. This, then, provides us with a valuable environmental datum upon which we can hang our interpretation of the other, related facies, or formations.

We can recognize an important ecological gradient paralleling the rapid increase in diversity of marine fossils as we proceed from the Manlius Formation eastward into the laterally equivalent units. Whereas the tidal-flat portion of the Manlius Formation has 5 to 10 species, subtidal Manlius rocks have 25 to 30, the Coeymans Formation 50 to 80, and the Kalkberg and New Scotland formations over 300 species. Surely this increase in diversity must indicate an increasingly more normal marine environment eastward of the Manlius environment, one in which variations in salinity, nutrients, water circulation, and so on were less frequent and less drastic.

Algal stromatolites in some Manlius facies further support a tidal-flat origin for parts of the Manlius Formation. The presence of calcareous algae in other Manlius strata argue for waters shallow enough to permit penetration of sunlight. Yet these waters must not have had strong, through-going currents, because Manlius rocks have a carbonate-mud matrix.

The next seaward facies, however, is mud-free; the calcareous silt and sand grains of the Coeymans Formation—mostly skeletal debris—are cemented by secondarily precipitated calcite within their interstices. The abundant attached echinoderms, or pelmatozoans, including crinoids and cystoids, lived with their feeding parts elevated off the seafloor by a stalk or stem. Tabulate corals and robust rooted brachiopods also thrived here. Whereas all other Helderberg facies are well burrowed, the Coeymans is much less so; but it does have good cross-stratification generated by strong currents. In short, then, we can interpret this facies as a more open, high-energy marine environment.

The next two seaward facies of the Kalkberg and New Scotland formations are similar in the abundance and diversity of Devonian marine invertebrates they include, and in their muddy and well-burrowed sediments. However, while the Kalkberg Formation is a quite pure limestone, the New Scotland Formation contains varying amounts of quartz silt and clay, presumably derived from erosion of lands still much farther to the east. The abundant and burrow-mottled mud, lack of primary current structures, and good marine fauna suggest an open, normal marine environment below wave base. As shown in Fig. 7-4, if we imagine a transgressing sea, we can visualize how these facies would migrate inland, with each seaward facies being deposited on the more inshore, adjacent facies. Over time, then, the vertical stratigraphic section that we call the Helderberg Group would build up from the laterally equivalent migrating facies.

LATEST JURASSIC ALLUVIAL PLAIN
OF THE WESTERN INTERIOR

After several major incursions of shallow seas from the North Pacific across what is now Canada, the western interior of the United States became dry land during the last stage of the Jurassic period owing to uplift from the Nevadan orogeny. Subsequent erosion of these ancestral Rocky Mountains at this time (about

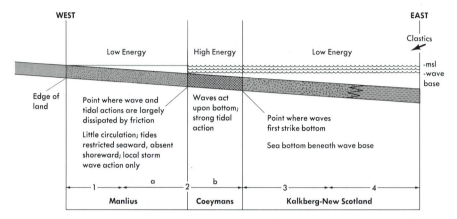

FIG. 7-4 Cross section of the sea in central New York during Early Devonian time, based upon facies analysis of the Helderberg Group. Numbered depositional environments include tidal flat (1), protected subtidal (2a), open subtidal and above wave base (2b), open subtidal and below wave base without terrigenous influx (3), and open subtidal and below wave base with terrigenous influx (4). Compare this figure with Table 7-1. The vertical scale is greatly exaggerated; water depths were several tens of meters at most, whereas the horizontal dimension of the figure is some 100 kilometers or more. (After L. F. Laporte, 1969.)

150 million years ago) resulted in the accumulation of widespread nonmarine alluvial deposits eastward, from Montana and North Dakota in the north, to Arizona and New Mexico in the south (Fig. 7-5). The sedimentary unit thus formed, the Morrison Formation, comprises various terrestrial facies, including fluvial gravels

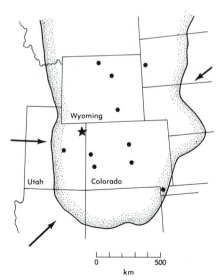

FIG. 7-5 Map of the Western Interior of the United States showing the distribution of Late Jurassic Morrison Formation. Dots are major dinosaur-collecting localities; star indicates Dinosaur National Monument, whose museum encloses exposed Morrison bone-bearing strata. Arrows show general source areas for the alluvial plain that formed the Morrison Formation. (After P. Dodson and others, 1980.)

and sands, floodplain muds, and freshwater swamp and pond deposits. The Morrison Formation is best known for its extremely abundant dinosaur fossils and consequently provides us with one of the best views of the Mesozoic reptilian world. Although for years a number of assumptions were made about this world, it is only recently that the paleoecology of the Morrison Formation has been studied in sufficient detail for us to have a clear picture of this ancient community and the habitat in which it lived. The following discussion is based chiefly on the results of a study undertaken by a team of vertebrate paleontologists, taphonomists, and sedimentologists to determine how the great creatures whose huge bones litter the Morrison lived, died, and were buried.

Stratigraphy and Facies

The Morrison Formation has a maximum thickness of a few hundred meters and covers an area of some 1 million square kilometers (about 380,000 square miles). It has been described by various field geologists as "uniformly variable." That is, it represents a variety of sedimentary environments, associated with a broad alluvial plain, uniformly throughout its thickness. Despite this variety, it is possible to recognize within the Morrison four major facies, based on sediment grain size, color, primary structures, and lateral relations. *Channel sands* are coarse, cross-stratified sand lenses, often with carbonate nodules and mud clasts reworked from surrounding contemporary sediments, that record river-channel erosion and sedimentation. *Oxidized floodplain mudstones* are silts and clays from overbank flooding of nearby rivers, with bioturbated bedding from burrowing animals and rooting plants as well as some paleosols (ancient soil horizons with carbonate nodules and iron concretions), usually colored red or brown from oxidation. *Reduced* floodplain mudstones are transitional from previous facies, with more clay, less silt in gray and green mudstones, better preserved laminated bedding, and less bioturbation, implying wetter conditions and a higher water table, although the occasional presence of mud cracks and reworked clasts indicates some periodic exposure. *Lacustrine limestones and marls* are thin, laterally persistent freshwater limestones and limy mudstones with occasional stromatolites and charophytes (reproductive organs of freshwater algae), mud cracks, and molluscs indicating larger ponds and lakes lying topographically lower in the alluvial plain.

These facies record a shifting complex of river and stream channels—some perennial, most ephemeral—interfingering laterally with their floodplains, usually well drained, but sometimes low enough to hold standing water for longer periods of time (Fig. 7-6). The nodular paleosols, mud cracks, and absence of coaly strata indicate a semiarid climate, with heavy seasonal rainfall to support the vegetation necessary to feed the large numbers of huge plant-eating dinosaurs. From several indirect sources of dating, these environments within the Morrison appear to have lasted about 10 million years.

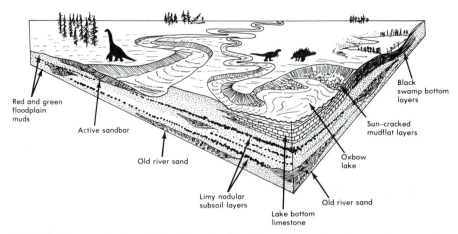

FIG. 7-6 Reconstruction of Morrison showing the major sedimentary environments of river channel, floodplain, and local bodies of fresh water. As the region subsided, the alluvial sediments accumulated, with the various environments migrating across the area, building up a complex three-dimensional pile of "variably uniform" nonmarine sediments. From time to time dinosaurs and other land-dwelling vertebrates died and were buried within the accumulating pile of strata. (After R. Bakker, copyright ©1986, by permission of William Morrow & Company.)

Vertebrate Fossils

More than a century ago, when the transcontinental railroad was being built, excavations along the right-of-way uncovered a number of huge bones from a variety of dinosaurs. So abundant were these remains that in one remote locality a sheepherder had fashioned himself a simple shelter using the bones like logs! And so unusual were the fossils that a number of expeditions put out from the East Coast to recover them, leading to the infamous O. C. Marsh–E. D. Cope competition that made headline news in the late nineteenth century.

Over a dozen genera of dinosaurs have been recovered from the Morrison, including the large sauropod herbivores *Apatosaurus, Camarasaurus,* and *Diplodocus,* the herbivorous ornithopods *Stegosaurus* and *Camptosaurus,* and the predatory theropods *Allosaurus* and *Ceratosaurus* (Fig. 7-7). Besides these attention-getting behemoths, the Morrison contains other interesting fossils, including frequent smaller dinosaurs the size of ostriches as well as subadults and juveniles of the large species; occasional crocodiles, turtles, lungfishes, and freshwater clams and snails; scattered primitive mammals (mostly teeth and jaws) the size of small rodents; and rare plant fragments. There are also abundant isolated tracks as well as some dinosaur trackways, the latter of which suggest herding behavior—juveniles and subadults in the center of the herd, adults around the perimeter. However, the large dinosaurs do predominate as fossils, in part because of original conditions— there was not enough permanent water to support an abundant community of turtles, crocodiles, and amphibians—and in part from postmortem taphonomic loss—trampling by the large herds of big animals destroyed the bones of smaller animals, like

FIG. 7-7 Morrison dinosaur community. From left to right: the predator *Allosaurus*, (planning dinner) and the herbivores *Camarasaurus* (walking), *Diplodocus* (drinking), and *Stegosaurus* (looking). All these dinosaurs were a few tens of feet in length and several tens of tons in weight. (Drawing by Gregory S. Paul; from *Earth and Life through Time*, by Steven M. Stanley. Copyright © 1986 W. H. Freeman and Company. Reprinted with permission.)

those of the primitive mammals, beyond recognition. (Recall our discussion of sheep and coyote bones in Chapter 5.)

The dinosaurs occur in repeated, localized concentrations of bones (some skulls and teeth, too), containing tens of individuals. Some of these concentrations are the slow accumulation of bones over a number of seasons or years in a stream channel or on the floodplain; others are the victims of mass mortalities from flash flooding or from the sudden miring of a herd in a shallow lake or muddy bog. In most cases, whatever the cause of death, the remains are usually disarticulated, indicating subsequent scavenging and trampling of the skeletons as they lay about on the sediment surface for some time before final burial.

Paleoecology

The facies distribution of the six most common genera of Morrison dinosaurs demonstrates that they probably inhabited all parts of the alluvial plain more or less equally (Fig. 7-8), although there is some tendency for the fossils in be preferentially collected in the higher-energy portion of the habitat. Whereas channel sands account for only 15 percent of the Morrison section, they contain more than one-third of the dinosaur bones. The data in Figure 7-8 also suggest that *Stegosaurus* may have been a more marginal member of the community, perhaps preferring the drier upland. This idea is supported by the fact that no *Stegosaurus* tracks have been found; drier upland surfaces would not easily record footprints. Note, too, that the lacustrine environment has the least number of dinosaur remains, compared with the

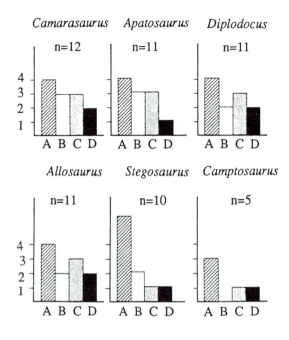

FIG. 7-8 Histograms showing the general evenness of distribution of the six most common dinosaurs in the four major facies of the Morrison. (A) channel sands; (B) and (C) oxidized and reduced floodplain mudstones, respectively; and (D) freshwater limestones and marls. This evenness of distribution suggests that they were all members of a single community that ranged widely across the Morrison alluvial plain, although *Stegosaurus* was perhaps a somewhat more marginal member of the community. Note that the sauropods (*Camarasaurus, Apatosaurus, Diplodocus*), despite their great bulk, are not restricted to the aquatic facies (D). (From P. Dodson and others, 1980.)

other environments, contradicting the long-held view that these huge animals could support their bulk only in large bodies of water.

Can we further infer what sort of habitat the Morrison alluvial plain might have been? Figure 7-9 compares the distribution of selected vertebrates from Pleistocene terrestrial deposits in Kenya with those from the Morrison Formation. We see that the facies distribution of *Diplodocus* and *Camarasaurus* is most like that of the elephant, whereas *Stegosaurus* is more comparable to the rhinoceros. Moreover, the dinosaurs do not show facies distributions that are similar to semiaquatic (e.g., hippopotamus) or fully aquatic (e.g., crocodiles, turtles) vertebrates, again contradicting earlier speculation that the large sauropods lived in water.

A final conclusion of the Morrison study is that, given the large size and abundance of the herbivores and assuming that the climate was one of seasonal rather than year-round rainfall, then the dinosaurs must have been migratory, moving from place to place to find adequate vegetation (Fig. 7-10). Such seasonal migrations by large herds of terrestrial vertebrate herbivores is, of course, the situation today on the East African Serengeti Plain. That conclusion further implies that dinosaurs must have been metabolically quite active to accomplish such wide-ranging migration—hardly the sluggish layabouts that they are sometimes assumed to have been.

MIOCENE OFFSHORE BASINS OF CALIFORNIA

In coastal California the Monterey Formation of Miocene age is several thousands of meters thick and records deposition in offshore fault-basins. The formation is of special interest because it produces more than 50 percent of

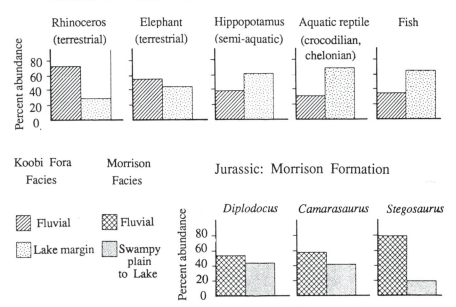

FIG. 7-9 Comparison of terrestrial vertebrates from the Morrison Formation with those from the Pleistocene Koobi Fora Formation of Kenya, showing percentage of habitat preference of individual taxa. Although the sedimentary environments of the two formations are not identical, they can be similarly subdivided into fluvial and lake margin (Koobi Fora) and fluvial and swampy plain to lake (Morrison). Note the comparable distributions for elephants and the sauropods (*Diplodocus* and *Camarasaurus*) and for rhinoceroses and the ornithopod *Stegosaurus*. (From P. Dodson and others, 1980.)

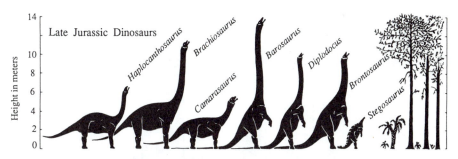

FIG. 7-10 Morrison herbivorous dinosaurs drawn to scale showing how size and feeding posture of various genera took advantage of the availability of food on plants of differing heights. A very similar situation exists among the diverse modern herbivores of the Serengeti Plain, which range in size, for example, from giraffe, elephant, and rhino to wildebeest, gazelle, zebra, and dik-dik. (From R. Bakker, copyright ©1986, by permission of William Morrow & Company.)

California's oil and contains an estimated 12 billion barrels of oil, much of it on the outer continental shelf.

The Monterey is a *hemipelagic* sedimentary rock, that is, a combination of pelagic biogenic particles (calcareous and siliceous plankton) and fine-grained clastics (silt and clay) deposited along continental margins, usually in deeper, offshore water. Rates of sedimentation for hemipelagic sediments are several tens to hundreds of centimeters per 1,000 years because of the higher biological productivity of coastal waters and greater influx of land-derived sediments. In contrast, open-ocean, *pelagic* deposits are mostly biogenic, forming in areas of lower productivity and with greatly reduced terrigenous clastics; thus, their sedimentation rates are usually only 1 to 2 centimeters per 1,000 years.

Stratigraphy and Facies

The Monterey Formation spans the early Miocene to latest Miocene (22 to 5 million years ago) and forms the sedimentary fill in some half-dozen basins generated by localized rifting along opposing sides of the San Andreas strike-slip fault system, which marks the plate boundary between the North American and Pacific plates. The Monterey's lithology varies from a coccolith-rich, calcareous facies in the lower part to a diatom-rich, siliceous facies in the upper part (Fig. 7-11). Coccolithophorids—

FIG. 7-11 The Miocene Monterey Formation in the Coastal Ranges of California as a record of basin formation and subsidence owing to tectonic activity along the San Andreas Fault. The Monterey change from calcareous coccolith-rich to siliceous diatom-rich facies also records South Polar refrigeration during the shift from a nonglacial to glacial world in mid-Miocene time. (After K. A. Pisciotto and R. E. Garrison, 1981.)

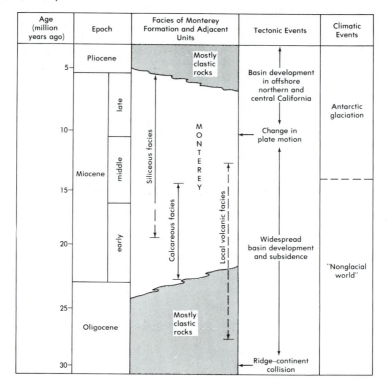

coccoliths—are calcareous phytoplankton belonging to the golden brown algae, usually 5 to 10 microns in diameter; diatoms are also phytoplanktonic golden brown algae, but with opaline silica tests that are quite variable in size from a few microns up to 2,000 microns (2 millimeters) in diameter (Fig. 7-12(A, B)). Both coccoliths and diatoms are important components in present-day plankton, but coccoliths are relatively more abundant in waters of lower nutrients, and diatoms more abundant in waters of higher nutrients (Fig. 7-12(C)). The tests of both accumulate on the seafloor as they settle down through the water column after death, either in the fecal pellets of animals higher in the food chain that graze on the phytoplankton or in mucus-bound films of fine-grained organic detritus that drift in the water column, so-called marine snow.

Besides differences in initial abundance owing to the varying fertility of the local waters, there are also preservational differences between these two kinds of phytoplankton. Calcareous coccoliths are readily dissolved below the CCD (refer to discussion of pelagic facies in Chapter 3), but siliceous diatoms are not. Thus, in nutrient-rich waters where the seafloor lies below the CCD, diatoms will accumulate in great abundance, whereas in waters of lower fertility and where the seafloor lies above the CCD, coccoliths will accumulate more abundantly.

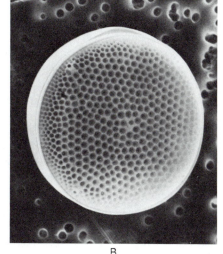

A   B

FIG. 7-12 Scanning electron microphotograph of a coccolith (A, × 5000) and a diatom (B, × 4000). Graph (C) shows results of culture experiment in which modern species of coccolithophore and diatom vary in growth rate as nitrate concentration increases. (A and B from Marcia Gowing, Institute of Marine Sciences, University of California, Santa Cruz; C after R. W. Eppley, 1970, Relationships of phytoplankton species distribution to the depth distribution of nitrates, *Bulletin Scripps Institute of Oceanography*, vol. 17, p. 43.)

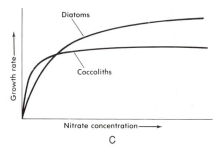

C

Paleoecology

At the beginning of Monterey deposition (which started at somewhat different times in different basins, between 22 to 18 million years ago), earlier movements along the San Andreas Fault had formed a series of rift basins arranged in a more or less north-south direction along the western edge of what is present-day California. The basins, separated from direct connection to the land, were thus sheltered in varying degrees from most land-derived erosional debris, although fine-grained silt and clay in suspension did reach them. The ocean waters were also removed from direct land-runoff of nutrients, so that a community of coccoliths (and some foraminiferans) flourished. The resulting calcareous hemipelagic sediments accumulated in the basins throughout early and part of middle Miocene time.

In the middle Miocene, some 16 to 14 million years ago, the Monterey sediments became diatom-rich, indicating a shift to more nutrient-rich waters. Current researchers believe that increased upwelling along the Pacific Coast must have brought more nutrients, especially nitrates, from deep levels (hundreds of meters) of the ocean (where the nutrients are released from decomposing organic matter) into surface waters, so that the diatoms proliferated at the expense of the coccoliths. For the rest of Miocene time, until 5 million years ago, thick diatomaceous strata of the Monterey were deposited. But what was the cause of this intensified upwelling that permitted the shift from coccolith to diatom dominance in the phytoplankton?

The answer is provided by eastern Pacific deep-sea cores, which span much of Miocene time but which were collected farther offshore than the Monterey Formation. Oxygen isotope studies of the calcium carbonate tests of the benthic foraminifer *Cibicidoides* from these cores indicate a sharp decline in bottom-water temperature, from relatively warm to colder water during the middle Miocene, 15 to 12 million years ago, coinciding with the shift from coccolith to diatom sedimentation in the Monterey (Fig. 7-13). We also know from other paleoclimatic data from around the world that during the mid-Miocene there was major global cooling that was related to continued breakup of the old Mesozoic supercontinents of Laurasia in the Northern Hemisphere and Gondwana in the Southern Hemisphere. One important consequence of this climatic cooling was South Polar refrigeration that resulted in widespread continental glaciation on the Antarctic landmass as well as chilling of the surrounding surface waters of the Antarctic Ocean. These chilled surface waters increased in density, both from cooling and from the rise in salinity accompanying the formation of sea ice. The dense surface waters then sank to deeper levels in the Antarctic Ocean and spread northward into the Atlantic, Indian, and Pacific oceans, thereby intensifying oceanic circulation and, in particular, increasing the strength of upwelling waters along the California coast. Global cooling, in general, would also favor increased oceanic circulation and upwelling owing to the steepening of latitudinal temperature gradients from the poles to the equator, with a consequent increase in atmospheric circulation, whose stronger surface winds would stir the upper layers of the oceans more intensely.

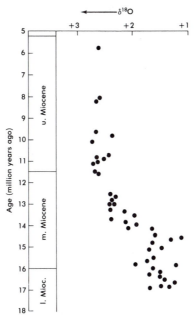

FIG. 7-13 Oxygen isotope measurements from the test of the benthic foraminifer *Cibicidoides* from three cores in the eastern Pacific that span the Miocene, where

$$\delta^{18}O = \left(\frac{^{18}O/^{16}O \text{ sample} - {^{18}O/^{16}O} \text{ standard}}{^{18}O/^{16}O \text{ standard}} \right) \times 1000$$

Note the sharp increase in the heavy ^{18}O during the mid-Miocene, from 15 to 12 million years ago. (After E. Barrera and others, 1985. Geological Society of America Memoir 163, p. 89.)

Antarctic cooling in mid-Miocene time was thus recorded thousands of miles away in the oxygen isotopes of open-ocean, bottom-dwelling foraminifera, like *Cibicidoides,* and in Monterey Formation facies changes from coccolith- to diatom-dominated sediments in the offshore basins of California.

PLEISTOCENE DEEP SEA OF THE NORTH ATLANTIC

The North Atlantic Ocean has formed over the last 200 million years, starting with the breakup of Pangaea, a large supercontinent composed of essentially the present-day dispersed continents, in Late Triassic time. Rifting and continuous divergence of the western and eastern portions of the northern part of Pangaea—so-called Laurasia—led to the opening of the North Atlantic Ocean, formation of the broad midoceanic volcanic ridges, lateral migration of the seafloor from opposite sides of the diverging plate boundary, and sedimentation of a relatively thin layer of pelagic deposits on the underlying submarine volcanics that accumulated along the ridge axis.

Much of the coarser, land-derived detritus that is brought to the ocean accumulates on the continental shelves, which are rather wide areas of little relief that extend seaward from land down to about 200 meters. In addition, turbidity currents occasionally transport relatively coarse sediments from the shelf edge, or down the submarine canyons that incise the shelf, and deposit them out on the abyssal plains.

Besides these inorganically derived deposits, there is also a significant amount of biogenic sediment accumulating in the more offshore and deeper parts of the ocean, out on the abyssal plains, away from the continental shelves and slopes. These pelagic sediments come mainly from calcareous planktonic foraminifera and coccoliths; other less important skeletal remains include the shells of planktonic snails (pteropods), various invertebrates, and fish debris.

In the two decades after World War II, when oceanographic research expanded greatly, hundreds of sediment cores from the abyssal plains of the North Atlantic were taken. These cores of soft sediment, most of which are 10 meters or more in length, provide a stratigraphic record of deep-sea geologic history. Although most of the cores record only the Holocene and Pleistocene interval, about 10 percent sample pre-Pleistocene sediments, some even going as far back as the Cretaceous period. These older sediments at or near the seafloor's surface are due to the nondeposition or erosion of younger sediments.

Qualitative Environmental Changes

Because of the abundance of planktonic Foraminifera in these cores, and because these single-celled organisms are sensitive to variations in water temperature, it was quickly realized that differences in the foraminiferal species in the cores might provide clues about the ancient temperature of the North Atlantic, particularly during the Pleistocene epoch, when significant warming and cooling of the earth's surface occurred.

The scientists studying these cores reasoned that first it would be necessary to determine which planktonic foraminifera were accumulating in the ocean sediments today, a "warm" interval. Obviously, benthic foraminifera would not be helpful, for their distribution, if it is related to temperature, would be controlled by the temperatures prevailing at several thousand meters rather than by surface temperature. And yet surface temperature, of course, would be far more sensitive to major climatic changes than would the bottom waters of the North Atlantic.

By defining the planktonic foraminiferal composition of the uppermost layer of the cores, it would be possible to establish a reference point, or environmental datum, with which other, older assemblages might be compared. For example, one foraminiferal species, *Globorotalia menardii,* is a useful indicator for determining surface temperature because this species, which fluctuates in abundance in the calcareous layers of the cores, is strongly influenced by temperature. In the uppermost layers of the North Atlantic cores *G. menardii* is abundant; going down the core, however, this species disappears for a time and then reappears once again. This variation in *G. menardii* was attributed to the end of the last glacial age and the beginning of the recent episode of marine sedimentation and climatic amelioration. To judge from the *G. menardii* foraminiferal populations, therefore, a warm, preglacial interval was followed by a cold period (glacial interval) without *G. menardii*, which was followed by another warm period (postglacial) with *G. menardii* again (Fig. 7-14).

Besides *G. menardii*, some 15 to 20 other planktonic foraminiferal species and subspecies are used to define the deep-sea Pleistocene and Holocene stratigraphy of the North Atlantic. But once the sequence of foraminiferal assemblages in any one core is established, it is necessary to correlate it with the sequences established in other cores. The reason for this is that none of the cores contains a continuous record of the Pleistocene epoch. These hiatuses are due to submarine slumping, submarine erosion, or nondeposition.

One useful method for correlating cores is based on a surprising phenomenon: Some foraminiferal species apparently change their direction of coiling with changes in water temperature. For example, *Globigerina pachyderma*, the only planktonic foraminifer living in the Arctic Ocean, coils to the left. But farther south, in subarctic waters of the North Atlantic it coils to the right. In this species, at least, coiling direction is dependent on water temperature (Fig. 7-15). A second species of foraminifer, *Globorotalia truncatulinoides*, also changes its direction of coiling from cold to warm surface waters, except this species coils to the left in warmer waters and to the right in colder waters, just the converse of *G. pachyderma*. Why these coiling directions occur is not known; nevertheless, it has been shown empirically that they are indeed correlated with temperature changes.

Further support for the conclusion that relative abundance of *G. menardii* and coiling direction of foraminifera mark changes in Pleistocene water temperatures of the North Atlantic is provided by oxygen isotopes. It has been observed that the relative amount in seawater of two isotopes of oxygen, ^{18}O and ^{16}O, varies with water temperature (refer to Chapter 6). Planktonic foraminifera, in secreting their calcium carbonate shells, use the oxygen isotopes in the same proportion as in the surrounding seawater. Thus, shells secreted in colder water have a relatively higher ratio of ^{18}O to ^{16}O than do tests secreted by these same organisms in warmer water. The occurrence of these isotopic relationships in foraminiferans in North Atlantic cores agrees with the warm-cold intervals determined by *G. menardii* abundance ratios and by reversals in coiling directions of *G. truncatulinoides* and *G. pachyderma* (Fig. 7-16).

Reasoning from the recent to the past allows us to map the species composition of planktonic foraminifera characteristic of present-day polar, subpolar, subtropical, and tropical water masses of the North Atlantic based on their occurrences at the tops of deep-sea cores. Knowing then which assemblage of species lives in which water mass today, we can measure their relative abundances downward in these same cores to see how the position of the water masses may have varied in the past. As shown in Fig. 7-17, the position of the subpolar assemblage of foraminifera was much farther south during the peak of the last ice age, some 18,000 years ago.

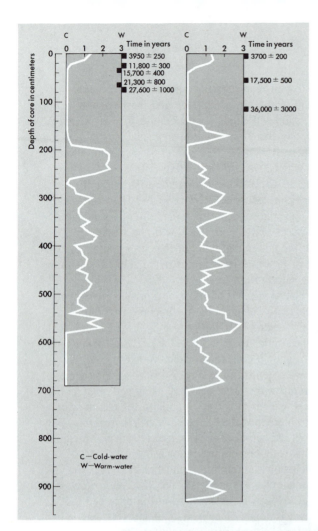

Time in years (left core):
3950 ± 250
11,800 ± 300
15,700 ± 400
21,300 ± 800
27,600 ± 1000

Time in years (right core):
3700 ± 200
17,500 ± 500
36,000 ± 3000

C—Cold-water
W—Warm-water

FIG. 7-14 Variations in abundance of the foraminifer *Globorotalia menardii* in two cores from the Caribbean. The curves record changing ratios of *G. menardii* to weight of sediment coarser than 74 micrometers; low ratios indicate colder water temperatures, higher ratios, warmer water (ratios shown at top of columns). Cold intervals do not occur at the same exact depth in the cores owing to varying rates of sedimentation in the two cores. Dates to right of each core were obtained by ^{14}C method; note that since 10 to 15 thousand years ago the Caribbean has become warmer. Photograph (below) shows several specimens of *Globorotalia menardii* enlarged about 22 diameters. (Drawing from D. Ericson and others, 1961; photo from D. Ericson and G. Wollin, 1964.)

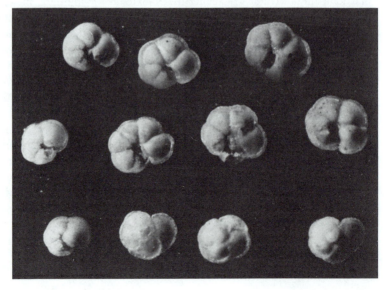

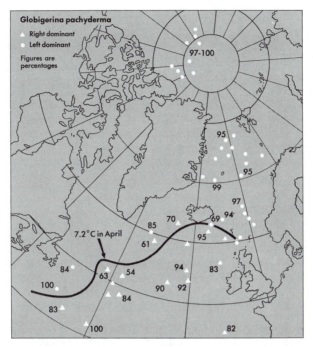

FIG. 7-15 Correlation between coiling direction of *Globigerina pachyderma* and surface water temperature. This foraminifer coils to the left in colder waters and to the right in warmer waters. The boundary between the two different populations parallels the 7.2°C April isotherm. (From D. Ericson and G. Wollin, 1964.)

Quantitative Environmental Changes

What we have just described are qualitative changes in environment, namely temperature, during late Pleistocene time in the North Atlantic. These changes in temperature are, of course, related to the waxing and waning of glaciation in the Northern Hemisphere as seen on the North American and European continents. The crucial, implicit assumption made in these qualitative changes in late Pleistocene paleoecology is that present-day marine species of plankton and their immediate Pleistocene ancestors respond identically to the marine ecology. That is, we have assumed that modern-day *G. menardii* and *G. pachyderma,* for example, respond to changes in water mass temperature just the way that the Pleistocene members of these same species did during the last several hundred thousand years of the late Pleistocene epoch. This assumption appears warranted, because the climatic results based upon these and other planktonic species are internally consistent and agree with other independent climatic indicators such as oxygen-isotope ratios.

More recently, paleoecologists have taken this assumption to its logical conclusion by *quantitatively* measuring past changes in North Atlantic water masses using temperature and salinity tolerances of many present-day species of marine plankton. This quantitative methodology includes the following procedures: deter-

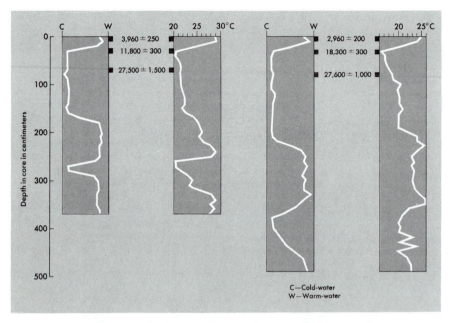

FIG. 7-16 Two cores from the North Atlantic Ocean showing close agreement in each of the climatic curves based on foraminferal assemblages and oxygen isotope ratios; absolute ages based on ^{14}C measurements are also given. Note that sediment accumulation rates in the upper part of each core are similar, but that in the lower portions (below 200 centimeters) the core on the right indicates somewhat more rapid accumulation of sediment. (D. Ericson and G. Wollin, 1961.)

FIG. 7-17 Relative abundances of recent foraminifera characterizing subpolar assemblages (A) and their distribution some 18,000 years ago, during the peak of the last ice age (B). Note the northward migration of the subpolar assemblage, no doubt due to the warming of the northern polar seas following glaciation. (After N. Kipp and others, 1976; A. McIntyre and others, 1976.)

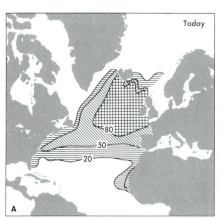
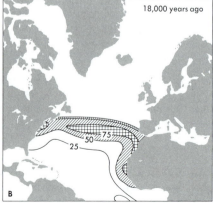

mining the present-day composition of plankton accumulating on the seafloor from a large number of locations in widely differing latitudes and longitudes; obtaining average winter and summer temperatures as well as average salinity of the surface waters for each of these locations; and then determining how the plankton changes in composition going downward in these same cores (Fig. 7-18). The changes in planktonic composition backward in time (going down the core) presumably reflect

FIG. 7-18 Quantitative estimates of temperature and salinity of Caribbean Sea water for the last one-half million years based on the relative abundances of planktonic foraminifera whose present-day temperature and salinity preferences are known. These estimates, based on a single core, are independently supported by oxygen isotope data from the tests of the same foraminifera. (After J. Imbrie and N. Kipp, 1971.)

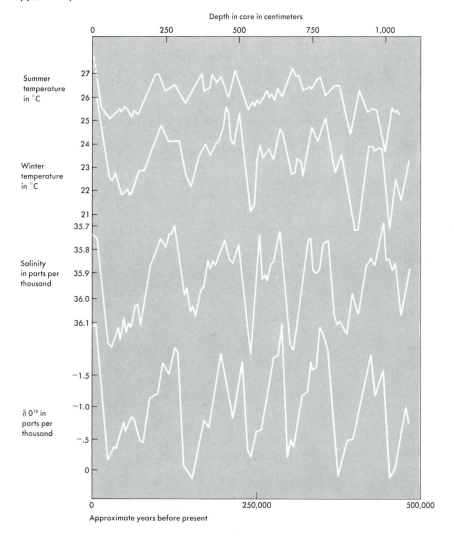

Depth in core in centimeters

Summer temperature in °C

Winter temperature in °C

Salinity in parts per thousand

δO^{18} in parts per thousand

Approximate years before present

corresponding changes in temperature and salinity of the overlying water mass, as-suming that the plankton are ecologically related to these environmental parameters.

This method has been applied to a long core from the Caribbean Sea, and quantitative systematic variations in temperature and salinity have been recorded for almost one-half million years at this one location (Fig. 7-18). Oxygen isotope data from the calcareous tests of these same microfossils strongly support the tempera-ture-salinity variations based solely on the faunal composition of the different levels in the core. As more and more such cores are studied, it becomes possible to con-tour temperatures and salinity values of the North Atlantic—and other oceans as well, as the methodology is extended—at specific times in the past (Fig. 7-19).

FIG. 7-19 Winter surface temperatures (degrees Celsius) for the North Atlantic Ocean during the last maximum glaciation, some 18,000 years ago. This map is based upon planktonic foraminifera and coccolithophorids found in North Atlantic cores at levels of this age and assumes that these planktonic microfossils had the same ecological requirements then as now. Compare this map with the distribution of the subpolar foraminiferal assemblage shown in Fig. 7-17 (B). Continental glaciers are shown by hachures, pack ice by stippling, and loose pack ice by triangles. Glacial shorelines are drawn using present bathymetry lowered by 100 meters. (After A. McIntyre and others, 1976.)

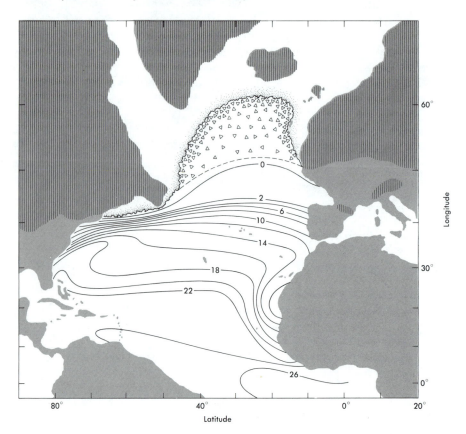

Milankovitch Cycles

One exciting and unexpected outcome of these measures of qualitative and quantitative environmental change has been the recognition of global climatic cycles over the last three-quarter million years. Major, long-term temperature changes in the surface waters of the North Atlantic Ocean presumably reflect worldwide climatic cycles that result from variations in Earth's eccentricity of orbit around the sun, in the inclination of Earth's axis of rotation, and in the precession of that axis. These astronomically induced, climatic cycles on Earth were first postulated earlier in this century by Milutin Milankovitch, who predicted that the solar heat received by Earth would fluctuate significantly owing to these cyclic changes (Fig. 7-20). One dramatic result of this fluctuating heating is periodic cold/warm cycles, expressed most recently in Earth history as glacial and interglacial stages of the Quaternary period.

The Milankovitch theory is that under certain orbital configurations, cool Northern Hemisphere summers allow an annual net increase in ice in high latitudes, because summer temperatures are not high enough to melt all the previous winter's snow, so it contributes to the following winter's ice pack. Thus, during an interval of cool northern summers, more and more ice accumulates until continental glaciers begin to form and flow southward. The glacial cycle ends when northern summers become warm enough to melt more snow and ice than was accumulated the previous winter, so that the glacial ice eventually melts away.

Verification of the Milankovitch theory has only recently come from the oxygen isotope record of low- and mid-latitude, near-surface-dwelling planktonic foraminifera in deep-sea cores. As glacial ice accumulates, seawater, which is the main reservoir for such ice, experiences an increase in its ^{18}O to ^{16}O ratio, because the lighter isotope evaporates more readily, so the snow that becomes glacial ice is isotopically lighter. But the marine calcareous plankton, which use the oxygen in seawater to build their tests, will have a correspondingly heavier isotopic composition during a cold (glacial) interval than during a warm (interglacial) interval, because of seawater's enrichment in ^{18}O. Thus, this hypothesis predicts a correlation between the fluctuating isotopic composition of calcareous tests, which record varying seawater temperatures, and the net amount of solar radiation received in high latitudes over time that results from changes in Earth's orbit. As Fig. 7-21 illustrates, this hypothesis is indeed borne out by the oxygen isotope data for the last 750 thousand years. Not only can we see what the climatic cycles of the recent geologic past have been, but we can also predict that Earth will be entering a new glacial climax about 22,000 years from now. The present has enabled us to interpret the past; and knowledge of the past now enables us to predict the future! (The "greenhouse effect" resulting from the increase of atmospheric carbon dioxide because of forest clearing and fossil fuel combustion may, in fact, counteract the future refrigeration of the globe as predicted by Milankovitch cycles. This greenhouse effect may in turn melt ice sheets, causing a global rise in sea level.)

Although there are many complicating factors, which we have not discussed here, there is general agreement that temporal fluctuations in the oxygen isotopes of

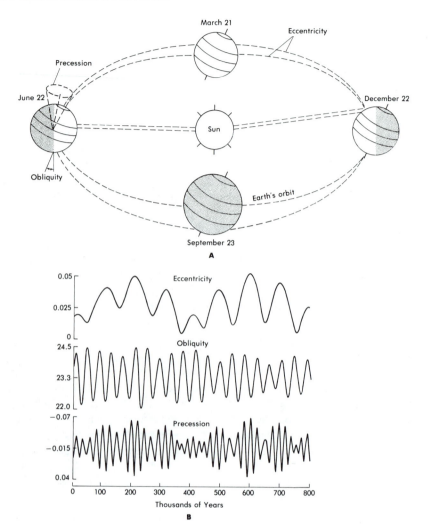

FIG. 7-20 Cyclic variations in Earth's orbital geometry. (A) Sketch illustrating changes in Earth's orbital geometry. (B) Cycles measured in years of amount of change in eccentricity, obliquity, and precession. Each of these variations influences the amount of solar radiation received at different Earth latitudes. Eccentricity measures the elliptical shape of Earth's orbit about the sun and varies on a 100,000-year cycle; obliquity, or "tilt," measures the degree of inclination from vertical of Earth's axis of rotation and varies on a 41,000-year cycle; and precession measures the wobble of the rotational axis and varies as a result of two component cycles, one at 23,000 years and a second at 19,000 years. The interaction of all these cycles produces a net cyclic change in the amount of heat received from the sun. Horizontal axis measured in hundreds of thousands of years; vertical axes measure (from top to bottom) proportional variations in Earth-sun distance, degrees from vertical of Earth's axis, and relative longitudinal position of spring equinox. (Reproduced by permission of the Geological Society from "A theoretical framework for the Pleistocene ice ages" by John Imbrie, in *Jour. Geol. Soc. London*, v. 142, 1985.)

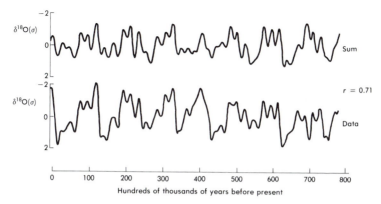

FIG. 7-21 Correlation between Milankovitch climatic cycles and oxygen isotopes over the last 750,000 years. The upper curve is a sum of the curves shown in Fig. 7-20(B) in terms of heat received by the earth, and the lower curve is an average of normalized oxygen isotope data from five low- and middle-latitude, deep-sea cores from the North Atlantic Ocean for two species of planktonic foraminifera. The horizontal scale is measured in hundreds of thousands of years. (Reproduced by permission of the Geological Society from "A theoretical framework for the Pleistocene ice ages" by John Imbrie, in *Jour. Geol. Soc. London,* v. 142, 1985.)

marine planktonic microfossils do indeed record the fluctuating accumulation of ice on the continents, which in turn is caused by variations in Earth's orbital geometry about the sun. We now have a strong working hypothesis for explaining Pleistocene glaciations, but there must be additional factors controlling glaciation, otherwise there should have been a continuous record of glacial/interglacial climate throughout geologic time. It may well be that while Milankovitch cycles can control continental glaciation, certain other conditions must first be met, like the size and latitudinal position of the continents. But even if periodic glaciation has not been constant over geologic time, other less dramatic climatic cycles on the Milankovitch scale, ranging from tens of thousands to hundreds of thousands of years, must be locked within the stratigraphic and paleontological record. Much paleoenvironmental research pursued today has as its goal the discovery of how these cycles manifest themselves within sedimentary rocks.

SUMMARY

The distribution and abundance of fossils can be explained in terms of the original ecological conditions of their ancient environments. In the case of older, mostly extinct biotas, we must rely heavily on the paleoenvironmental evidence provided by the enclosing sedimentary rocks. Environmental stratigraphy can therefore provide ecological understanding and insight, independent of the fossils themselves. Thus, the depositional environments for Early Devonian marine limestones and Late Jurassic nonmarine sandstones can be inferred from the lithofacies characteristics of these rocks. The knowledge of modern shallow carbonate and alluvial environments, respectively, can also shed light on the origin of these rocks. Having established the ancient habitats, it is then possible to relate specific fossil occurrences to them, in terms of the probable ways of life of the associated organisms, based on comparison with approximately similar adaptive types. Knowing the biological needs and ecological preferences of modern organisms like mat-building cyanobacteria, epifaunal suspension feeding brachiopods, or predatory lizardlike reptiles, we can reconstruct the ancient communities and ecosystems, at least in part.

When dealing with the much younger part of the fossil record, such as the Miocene and Pleistocene epochs, it may be feasible to use the ecology and biology of extant, living species to interpret past environments. Such a literal application of the "present is a key to the past" to deep-sea environmental conditions and, in turn, to global climate, may hold the answer to predicting future environmental conditions. Thus, we seem to be at an exciting threshold in the study of geologic history in general, and ancient environments in particular, namely, where we can look both backward and forward from our present instant in time and see the broad sweep of events—physical and biological—unfolding across the face of our planet, as a single, unified, and seamless time warp.

8

ENVIRONMENTS
IN CRISIS

Nevertheless so profound is our ignorance . . . and as we do not see the cause, we invoke cataclysms to desolate the world, or invent laws on the duration of the forms of life! (Charles Darwin. 1859. On the Origin of Species. London: John Murray, 73.)

The pace of ecological change in modern and ancient communities relates closely to the temporal stability of the environments they inhabit. We have already seen the responses of Devonian, Jurassic, Miocene, and Pleistocene biotic systems to areal and temporal variations in environment. Rapid environmental oscillations, such as those of the Pleistocene ice ages, trigger correspondingly frequent episodes of community replacement, in which cold-water floras and faunas replace warm-water biotas, and so on. In contrast to these Quaternary oscillations of environment and organisms, much of the geologic record indicates long intervals of mild, equable global climates, in which community replacement and community evolution proceeded at relatively slow rates.

During some intervals of Earth history, environmental stresses have been sufficiently severe or prolonged as to create widespread extinction and virtual collapse of the earth's major ecosystems. These episodes, called *mass extinctions,* represent important ecological and evolutionary "filters" that determine which species are available to form communities in later intervals. It is difficult even to comprehend the ecological severity of these events: For the most prominent mass extinctions, it has been estimated that 50 to 95 percent of all marine species were eliminated! Thus, the most severe mass extinctions not only greatly reduced global diversity but, more significantly, also altered the taxonomic and ecological composition of subsequent communities.

This final chapter considers the paleoecological significance of mass extinctions, with special emphasis on the following questions: How are mass extinctions recognized in the fossil record? Are mass extinctions periodic, with a predictable recurrence interval? What are the most likely causes of mass extinctions? As you will see, although much has been learned in recent years, many of the most interesting questions are still unresolved. Paleoecological and paleoenvironmental analyses of mass extinctions are current research frontiers in the earth sciences.

RECOGNITION OF MASS EXTINCTIONS

At any given time some groups of organisms on the planet are speciating, others are part of established species that are maintaining the status quo, and still others belong to species that are going extinct. As a consequence of this continuous turnover of species, our present biosphere comprises only a minute fraction (less than 0.01 percent) of all the species that have ever lived. Thus, in the words of one paleontologist, "Extinction is the normal way of life."

How, then, can we discriminate between this ongoing, "normal" extinction and mass extinctions? One approach is to examine extinction rates for a large segment of Phanerozoic history to identify normal (often termed *background*) extinction rates and compare them with exceptionally high, mass extinction rates. Such an approach is illustrated in Fig. 8-1, which shows the five major (first-order) mass ex-

FIG. 8-1 Major mass extinctions in the Phanerozoic history of life, expressed as total extinction rate (extinctions of families per million years) among marine vertebrates and invertebrates. The two dashed lines indicate levels of extinction within background or normal range; the spikes above background are the five major mass extinctions. Note that the background extinction rate has actually declined through geologic time. David Raup and John Sepkoski have inferred that this declining background extinction rate reflects an increasing evolutionary fitness for marine families over geologic time; however, as they note, this decrease in background extinction may also be an artifact of the fossil record. (From D. M. Raup and J. J. Sepkoski, 1982, *Science*, v. 215, p. 1501. Copyright 1986 by the AAAS.)

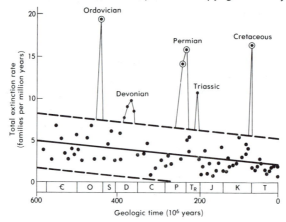

tinctions in the Phanerozoic marine animal record in comparison with background extinction rates bracketed by the dashed lines.

These most severe, first-order, mass extinctions in Ordovician, Devonian, Permian, Triassic, and Cretaceous time plot as anomalously high extinction rates, well above background levels. Figure 8-2 shows another compilation of these same data for marine families, illustrating the percentage decrease in diversity at each of these major extinctions. Note that the Permian event was by far the most severe mass extinction, with a loss of 52 percent of marine families.

FIG. 8-2 Phanerozoic compilation of diversity of marine vertebrate and invertebrate families. Note that the five major extinctions plot as significant valleys in the diversity curve. Percentages indicate the percentage loss of marine families for the major events. (From D. M. Raup and J. J. Sepkoski, 1982, *Science*, v. 215, p. 1502. Copyright 1982 by the AAAS.)

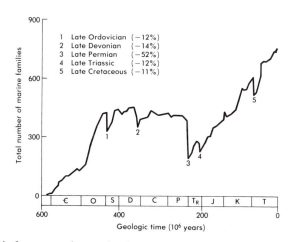

The ideal taxonomic unit for measuring extinction rates (in either modern or ancient studies) is, of course, the species. This is because, of all taxonomic levels, species correspond most nearly to real biological entities; whereas genera, families, orders, and so forth are taxonomic constructs designed to convey the evolutionary relationships among groups of species, the species is a group of organisms defined by distinct morphology and reproductive isolation from other groups of organisms. However, in paleontological compilations, lists of species for a given interval may be incomplete; for example, latest Ordovician brachiopods may be very well known, but contemporaneous bryozoans may be very poorly documented. Also, different workers may use different working definitions to discriminate species, resulting in a certain unevenness in species-level taxonomy. (This unevenness, by the way, exists in both biological and paleontological taxonomic studies, although biologists are better able to test their definitions of species operationally, by looking for interbreeding relationships among different populations.) Because of these uncertainties of species-level data and the vast numbers of species involved, most global diversity data for the fossil record are compiled using genera, families, or orders of organisms. Data on these higher taxonomic levels are probably more reliable and certainly more readily compiled. Figure 8-3 shows that extinction curves for different taxonomic levels (in this case, families and genera) are generally in agreement, although there may be minor differences.

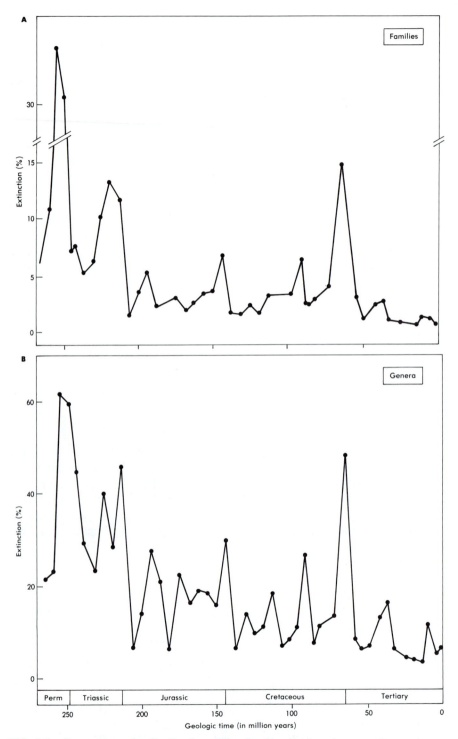

FIG. 8-3 Percentage of extinction for marine families (top) and genera (bottom) during the last 250 million years. Note the excellent correspondence of the two curves. (From D. M. Raup and J. J. Sepkoski, 1986, *Science,* v. 231, p. 834. Copyright 1986 by the AAAS.)

TIMING OF MASS EXTINCTIONS

One obvious feature of the five first-order mass extinctions (Figs. 8-1 and 8-2) is the tendency for these events to coincide with the terminal portions of geologic periods; extinctions occur at or very near the ends of the Ordovician, Permian, Triassic, and Cretaceous periods. The reason for this curious trend is, of course, that the early geologists who constructed various portions of the geochronologic scale based their subdivisions on major stratigraphic discontinuities and on faunal distinctions. Thus, the stratigraphic and faunal breaks associated with mass extinctions proved useful in subdividing the geologic column.

In addition to the first-order mass extinctions, extinctions that may be either global or only regional in scope have also been identified as lesser, or second-order extinctions. Figure 8-3 illustrates both first- and second-order mass extinctions for the last 250 million years (latest Paleozoic through Pleistocene). Because the second-order extinctions are less severe in terms of diversity loss, and because they may not have had global effects, recognition and timing of these events have proven more controversial than those of the first-order events.

Is there a periodicity in the timing of mass extinctions? Several recent studies claim that mass extinctions may be periodic on a scale of 26 to 32 million years, a proposal that has sparked controversy within the paleontological community. David Raup and Jack Sepkoski have presented arguments for an extinction periodicity of 26 million years, based upon the generic and familial diversity data illustrated in Fig. 8-3. This periodicity applies strictly to Mesozoic-Cenozoic extinctions, for when Paleozoic data are analyzed, longer periods result; also, Paleozoic data are apparently not as statistically reliable as for the Mesozoic-Cenozoic eras. Raup and Sepkoski have used the observed periodicities to argue for an extraterrestrial (impact) origin for mass extinctions. (We will discuss this link in further detail in the next section.)

The periodicity arguments have been debated widely, because of their importance in resolving possible causes of mass extinction. The most valid criticism of the periodicity model is that the observed periods may possibly be an artifact of the sampling intervals (stratigraphic stages) within the Mesozoic-Cenozoic record. As an example from the Paleozoic (rather than Mesozoic-Cenozoic), Fig. 8-4 shows that when sampled on a finer time scale, ammonoid cephalopods within the Famennian stage of the Late Devonian actually show a gradational pattern of family origination and extinction rather than a sudden extinction, as the stage-level data would suggest. Another argument against the periodicity model is that perhaps random processes may have produced extinction patterns such as those shown in Fig. 8-3—that is, the mass extinctions may be the result of coincidences of many normal, unrelated extinctions occurring close together in time. In any case, the hypothesis of a periodic pattern for extinction is an intriguing one that deserves further testing.

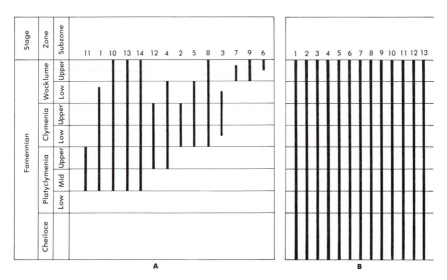

FIG. 8-4 Stratigraphic occurrence of clymeniid ammonoid cephalopods during the Famennian stage of the Late Devonian period. This chart shows the effect of the fine-scale sampling (A) versus stage-level sampling (B) of this group. When more detailed sampling was done, these ammonoids showed gradational origination and extinction patterns rather than the apparently instantaneous pattern provided by the relatively coarse, stage-level data. Numbers indicate various families within the order Clymeniida: 1, Hexaclymeniidae; 2, Costaclymeniidae; 3, Sellaclymeniidae; 4, Microclymeniidae; 5, Biloclymeniidae; 6, Wocklumeriidae; 7, Glatziellidae; 8, Gonioclymeniidae; 9, Parawocklumeriidae; 10, Cyrtoclymeniidae; 11, Rectoclymeniidae; 12, Carinoclymeniidae; 13, Clymeniidae; 14, Cymaclymeniidae. (From C. Teichert, 1986.)

CAUSES OF MASS EXTINCTIONS

Hypotheses to explain the origin of mass extinctions have proliferated in recent years, catalyzed by recent geochemical discoveries and by the claims for periodicity in extinctions. Some of the theories are specific to individual events or selected taxonomic groups, whereas other explanations present a unified model for all first- and second-order extinctions. We will not discuss group-specific models (such as the theory that the demise of dinosaurs relates to their difficulties in digesting the newly emerging flowering plants!). Instead, we focus attention on several hypotheses that have potential as unifying theories to account for mass extinctions in the fossil record. You should bear in mind, however, it may well turn out that no single theory can account for all extinctions and that instead every mass extinction has its own unique set of circumstances.

Lowering of Global Sea Level

Global declines in sea level have been proposed as a mechanism to account for drops in diversity associated with mass extinctions. Lowered sea level has a twofold effect on the marine diversity record. First, as sea level drops, the continental shelves are drained, reducing the habitable area for shallow marine organisms on continental margins and creating regional extinctions where these marine habitats are eliminated. Second, because sea level is lowered and widespread unconformities occur on continental margins, the volume of *preserved* marine sediment for the interval is relatively low. This low volume of preserved sediment leads to relatively low apparent diversities for the interval, as a taphonomic bias rather than a signal of true diversity levels (see section in Chapter 5 on taphonomic megabiases in the stratigraphic record).

Because several of the first-order extinctions correlate with low stands of sea level (most notably, the terminal Ordovician, Permian, and Cretaceous events), this model initially gained considerable acceptance. The Permian event, for example, is by far the most intense of the five major extinctions and also coincides with the lowest sea-level stand in the Phanerozoic record (see sea-level curve in Fig. 3-2; also Fig. 8-5). However, the sea-level model has several flaws that limit it as a unifying theory for mass extinctions.

One limitation of the sea-level model is that two of the first-order extinctions (Devonian, Triassic) do not correlate with significant lowerings of sea level. On the contrary, the Devonian extinction occurs at a time of impressive sea-level *rise,* and the latest Triassic extinction correlates with only a minor drop in global sea level. A further difficulty with the model is that it predicts that major sea level drops should correlate with mass extinctions in most (if not all) cases. In fact, the largest sea-level drop during Cenozoic time, which occurred during the late Oligocene epoch, did not produce a substantial marine extinction (see Fig. 8-3). Finally, perhaps the most serious challenge to the sea-level model is its failure to explain mass extinctions of terrestrial or pelagic marine biotas. We can therefore conclude that although some extinctions do correlate with sea-level low stands, a cause-and-effect relationship between sea-level lowering and mass extinction has not been established.

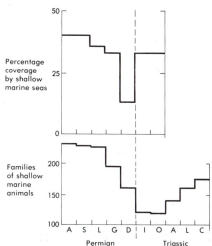

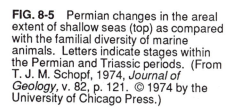

FIG. 8-5 Permian changes in the areal extent of shallow seas (top) as compared with the familial diversity of marine animals. Letters indicate stages within the Permian and Triassic periods. (From T. J. M. Schopf, 1974, *Journal of Geology,* v. 82, p. 121. © 1974 by the University of Chicago Press.)

Global Cooling

Steven Stanley, of Case Western Reserve University, has proposed that mass extinctions result from intense global-cooling events. He notes that climates during much of Earth history were warmer and much more equable than those of today; thermal contrasts between the poles and equator were very low during much of Phanerozoic time. In such a stable, aseasonal or only mildly seasonal world, the onset of glaciation or global cooling would have had severe effects on tropical and warm-temperate organisms, creating mass extinctions with most pronounced effects in low latitudes.

The most compelling evidence in support of this "refrigeration" theory of mass extinctions comes from the Paleozoic first-order extinctions. Both the Ordovician and Permian are intervals of major continental glaciations, comparable in scale to the Quaternary glaciations we discussed in Chapter 7. Some workers have also proposed a causal link between the Devonian extinction and possible Late Devonian continental glaciation in South America; however, the age of this glacial event is not well determined and may be of Carboniferous age instead.

A small-scale test of the global-cooling model can be found in Plio-Pleistocene faunal declines among benthic marine communities of the North Atlantic and Mediterranean regions. Stanley and coworkers have documented in these areas a regional mass extinction that correlated with introduction of cool currents into formerly tropical and subtropical habitats. Prior to the late Pliocene, rich molluscan faunas (with hundreds to more than a thousand species in each association) inhabited southeastern North America and the Mediterranean region. Then, approximately 3 million years ago, with the onset of Northern Hemisphere continental glaciation, changes in oceanographic circulation brought the cold Labrador Current southward along eastern North America, eliminating more than a thousand molluscan species from North Atlantic marine habitats. In the Mediterranean region a regional mass extinction also occurred during this interval, with approximately 40 percent of all shallow-water clam species eliminated.

Thus, the cooling theory finds support from both first-order extinctions and lesser, regional extinctions. However, some questions concerning this model still need to be clarified. Foremost among these is the issue of timing of extinctions relative to glaciations or cooling events. For example, the late Paleozoic glaciations have traditionally been considered Carboniferous to Early Permian in age, whereas the mass extinction is primarily Late Permian (see Fig. 8-3). A further, and critical, question is the extent to which cooling provides an explanation for the Mesozoic and Cenozoic mass extinctions. Also, is it possible to link climatic cooling with other causal mechanisms, such as meteorite impacts?

Meteorite Impacts

In 1978 Luis Alvarez and Walter Alvarez, along with coworkers at the University of California, Berkeley, discovered that the sediments of the Cretaceous-Tertiary boundary in Italy contained anomalously high concentrations of iridium, a platinum-group element that is depleted in Earth's crust but abundant in meteors and some other extraterrestrial bodies (Fig. 8-6). They later documented comparable iridium anomalies at sites in Denmark and New Zealand. In 1980 they proposed that the Late Cretaceous extinction resulted from a massive environmental disruption caused by the impact of a large meteorite (approximately 10 kilometers in diameter). Subsequently, this iridium anomaly at the Cretaceous-Tertiary boundary was recorded at more than 50 sites worldwide (Fig. 8-7) and was shown to be time-equivalent by biostratigraphic and magnetic correlation techniques.

In addition to iridium there are other indicators of meteorite impact at the Cretaceous-Tertiary boundary. Isotope abundances of another platinum-group ele-

FIG. 8-6 Iridium content of sediments straddling the Cretaceous-Tertiary boundary in the classic Gubbio stratigraphic section in Italy. Note the elevated concentration of iridium associated with the boundary. (From L. Alvarez, W. Alvarez, F. Asaro, and H. V. Michel, 1980, *Science*, v. 208, p. 1099. Copyright 1980 by the AAAS.)

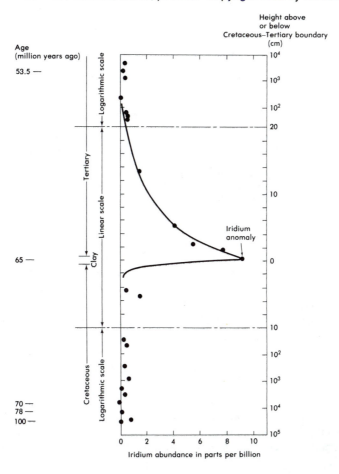

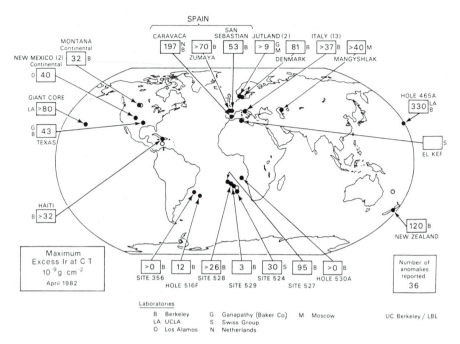

FIG. 8-7 Sites where the iridium anomaly is currently known to occur at the Cretaceous-Tertiary boundary and indications of some laboratories pursuing this work. The numbers indicate iridium concentrations in parts per billion; locations with anomalies whose curves are not yet well documented are labeled with concentrations > 0. Despite the very low abundances of iridium (parts per billion) in these samples, these values are considered anomalously high in comparison with the much lower concentrations typically found in the earth's crust. (From W. Alvarez and others, 1984, Geological Society of America Special Paper 190, Figure 1, p. 306.)

ment, osmium, further confirm the presence of meteoritic material. Quartz grains found in sediments at the boundary have fractures typical of deformation under such extremely high pressures that these textures are known only from extraterrestrial impacts (Fig. 8-8). Thus, diverse but convergent lines of physical evidence reinforce the impact interpretation of the iridium anomaly.

Could meteorite impacts be the cause of mass extinctions? An impact theory of mass extinctions has recently emerged, based on the documentation of an impact at the Cretaceous-Tertiary boundary along with evidence for extinction periodicity. One interpretation is that the 26 million year periodicity in the Raup and Sepkoski analysis records an astronomical cycle in which the biosphere is disrupted periodically by introduction of asteroidal or cometary material. For example, in the case of the Cretaceous-Tertiary boundary event (which we discuss more fully in the next section), many faunal and floral groups show marked diversity losses at or very near the stratigraphic level of the iridium anomaly. Precise environmental mechanisms

FIG. 8-8 Shocked quartz from the Lake Mitastin, Labrador, meteorite impact structure (1), compared with shocked quartz from a Cretaceous-Tertiary boundary section in Colorado (2). (Photograph by Glenn Izett, courtesy of Bruce F. Bohor, U.S. Geological Survey.)

for links between mass extinction and meteorite impact have not been fully worked out, although many models have called for darkening and cooling as a result of the particulate matter ejected into and above Earth's atmosphere following impact of a large meteorite (comparable to the object that formed the crater in Fig. 8-9). These models thus incorporate some elements of a global-cooling hypothesis, as discussed previously. However, alternative models suggest that intense environmental heating, rather than cooling, might result from a meteorite impact.

In addition to temperature changes, collision with a large asteroid would trigger even more dramatic environmental changes. For instance, dust particles introduced into the earth's atmosphere would cause a global darkening that might persist for months or even years; prolonged darkness would cause the shutdown of photosynthesis in both marine and terrestrial protists and plants. Another possible result of asteroid impact would be the formation of nitrous and nitric acids in the atmosphere, at levels high enough to acidify rainfall to pH levels of 0 to 1 (the worst acid rain in modern environments is between pH 3 and 4). An additional, even more speculative, proposal is that asteroid impact would have led to global forest fires. Thus, although the particular effects of impact are not fully known, many workers believe that collision with an asteroid or comet would have devastating environmental consequences.

Impact models for mass extinctions have gained increasing acceptance over the past few years but are still very controversial. One reason for the controversy is that, among the first-order extinctions, only the Cretaceous event has been linked with geochemical anomalies indicative of extraterrestrial influx. For example, extensive geochemical sampling of Devonian rocks has yielded slight iridium concentrations within stromatolitic rocks, but no global iridium anomaly has been discovered. Similarly, sampling across the Ordovician-Silurian boundary in Quebec and Scotland has not shown any spike of iridium indicative of an impact related to the terminal Ordovician extinction. However, it is also possible that some mass ex-

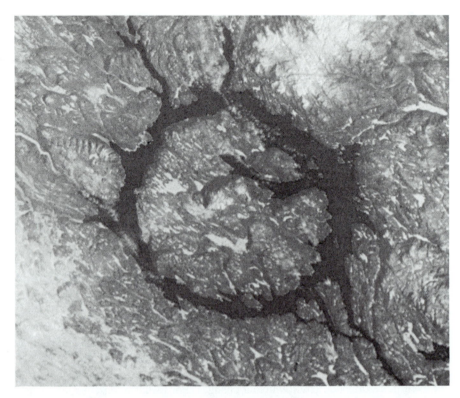

FIG. 8-9 The Manicouagan impact crater in Quebec. This impact structure has a diameter of 65 kilometers and is thought to be roughly contemporaneous with the Triassic-Jurassic boundary. Could this be related to the major extinction at the end of the Triassic period? (Photo courtesy of NASA.)

tinctions may have been caused by the impact of comets or some stony, achondritic meteorites that were not enriched in iridium and other platinum-group elements.

Another source of dispute is the discovery that some volcanic eruptions, such as those of the Hawaiian volcano Kilauea, contain unusually high levels of iridium. This has prompted some workers to propose a link between volcanism and mass extinction rather than between impact and mass extinction. Proponents of the impact theory have counterargued that the iridium levels from volcanic eruptions (0.32 parts per billion) are not sufficiently high to account for the global Cretaceous iridium anomaly (up to 340 parts per billion in some sites).

A CLOSER LOOK AT THREE MAJOR EXTINCTIONS

How can it be that such disparate hypotheses have been proposed as unifying theories for the extinctions? One source of controversy has been that the individual extinctions show differing patterns of diversity loss and environmental change. To illustrate this, we will take a closer look at three of the first-order events—the Ordovician, Permian, and Cretaceous mass extinctions.

Ordovician Mass Extinction

The Ordovician extinction involved such a large loss in marine diversity that some workers believe this to be the second most intense extinction in the Phanerozoic fossil record. Among approximately 100 marine families that perished during the extinction the groups most affected were the trilobites, cephalopods, brachiopods, and crinoids. Overall, 22 percent of all marine families died out, and for many groups the percentage loss of species may have been very high (for example, an estimated 60 percent of all brachiopod species went extinct). However, even these large numbers do not adequately reflect the severe ecological effects of the extinction, for many of the most abundant and widespread Ordovician species were eliminated during this event. The trilobites, for example, reached their maximum diversity during Ordovician time and were never again to regain previous diversity levels following the extinction. The effects of the Ordovician extinction are not evident in nonmarine environments; however, during this interval nonmarine faunas and floras are very poorly known (lake biotas are not widely preserved, and the radiation of plants and animals into terrestrial environments was, at most, in a very early phase).

A widespread continental glaciation correlates with the decline in faunal diversity during Late Ordovician time. Tropical, shallow-water marine groups were selectively extinguished, whereas high-latitude and deep-water organisms were affected relatively little. For these reasons many workers have called upon a glacial cooling model to account for the Ordovician event. Geochemical investigations of the two most complete Ordovician-Silurian stratigraphic sections in the world have disclosed no iridium anomaly or other evidence of a meteoritic impact coincident with the extinction.

Permian Mass Extinction

The Late Permian event ranks as the greatest of the Phanerozoic biological crises; diversity estimates suggest that approximately 50 percent of all marine families and up to 96 percent of all marine species were eliminated during Late Permian time. Among these, brachiopods, crinoids, corals, and cephalopods were the groups in which marine extinctions were greatest, though lesser extinctions occurred in a wide range of marine invertebrates. The groups selectively extinguished include many of the most abundant and characteristic biotas of the Paleozoic era: rugose corals, spiny brachiopods, large fusulinid foraminifera, and so forth. Also among the victims of the Permian event were groups such as trilobites, which had persisted through the late Paleozoic at relatively low diversities.

On land, too, the Permian event decimated a number of ecologically important groups of organisms. Among these terrestrial victims were the *therapsids,* mammal-like reptiles that may have been the most active of the late Paleozoic terrestrial carnivores. Several lines of evidence suggest that therapsids were warm-blooded (endothermic) and that they likely moved about energetically, consuming large quantities of prey. Thus, the extinction of most families of therapsids during the Late Permian event (Figs. 8-10 and 8-11) represented a fundamental ecological change in terrestrial ecosystems, even though most reptilian groups show relatively little diversity change during this interval.

Terrestrial plant communities were in a time of transition. During Late Permian time, the formerly dominant lycopods, sphenopsids, and cordaites dwindled in diversity, while seed plants increased correspondingly (Fig. 8-12). Overall, the species diversity of land plants decreased by approximately 20 percent during Permo-Triassic time, a significant diversity loss but not nearly so devastating as the extinctions in the marine realm.

Causes of the Permian extinction are still poorly understood, even though this was the most severe diversity loss in Phanerozoic history. As we discussed earlier, the Permian event does correlate with a sea-level low stand, although this factor alone is insufficient to account for the magnitude of the extinction. There also has been no solid evidence for meteorite impact. In fact, the protracted duration of the Permian diversity declines also argues against a short-lived, impact origin for the event. Of the major extinction hypotheses, the global-cooling model best explains the observed Permian trends, although as we noted earlier it is really not clear whether the timing of glaciation and extinction coincide.

Cretaceous Mass Extinction

As the most recent of the major mass extinctions, the Cretaceous event occupies a central position in any discussion of unifying causes. Compared with the other major extinctions, our ability to resolve small-scale time intervals and to correlate these intervals regionally and globally is far better for Cretaceous strata. Also, Cretaceous faunas and floras have closer counterparts among modern organisms than do the biotas of earlier periods; thus, the paleoecology of the Cretaceous extinction is far easier to interpret than those of the earlier events. For these reasons, patterns and processes of Cretaceous extinction have received much scrutiny.

In marine environments the terminal Cretaceous extinction eliminated 15 percent of all families and approximately 50 percent of the genera. Among benthic organisms the bivalves, gastropods, echinoids, and sponges were particularly severely affected. Extinction was also widespread among pelagic organisms; most species of cephalopods, planktonic foraminifera, and calcareous nannofossils suffered extinction, and fishes were also decimated. Within marine ecosystems the pace of extinction varied greatly, however. Some groups, such as articulate brachiopods, retained relatively constant diversity levels up to the Cretaceous-Tertiary boundary, whereas others, such as cephalopods, actually began to decline much earlier in the Cretaceous, so that by the end of the period there were relatively few remaining species killed off in the final event. This contrast in extinction rate is shown in Figs.

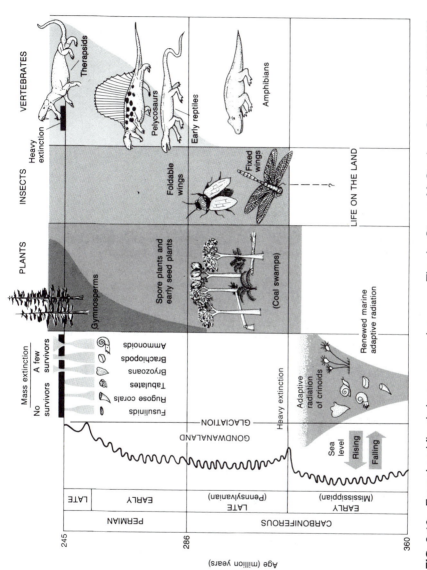

FIG. 8-10 Faunal and floral changes occuring during the late Paleozoic era, illustrating effects of the Late Permian extinction on marine and terrestrial biotas. (From *Earth and Life through Time* by Steven M. Stanley. Copyright © 1986 W. H. Freeman and Company. Reprinted with permission.)

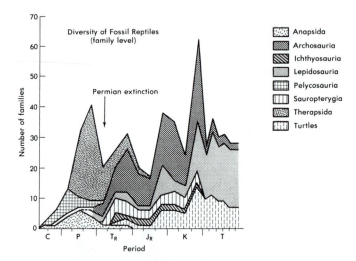

FIG. 8-11 Diversity of reptile families through time, illustrating major decline in therapsid families during the terminal Permian mass extinction. (From K. Padian and W. A. Clemens, 1985, in J. W. Valentine (ed.), *Phanerozoic Diversity Patterns: Profiles in Macroevolution,* Fig. 8, p. 57. Copyright © Princeton University Press. Reprinted with permission of Princeton University Press.)

FIG. 8-12 Species diversity within various groups of terrestrial plants during late Paleozoic and Mesozoic time. Note the late Paleozoic decline of the sphenopsids and lycopods and the corresponding increase in species diversity of seed plants. (From K. J. Niklas, B. H. Tiffney, and A. H. Knoll, 1985, in J. W. Valentine (ed.), *Phanerozoic Diversity Patterns: Profiles in Macroevolution,* Fig. 2, p. 107. Copyright © Princeton University Press. Reprinted with permission of Princeton University Press.)

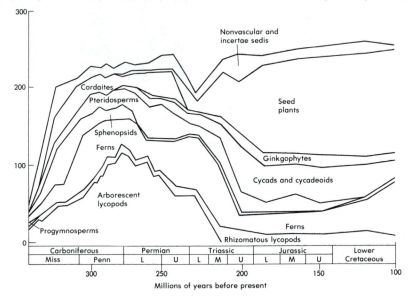

8-13 and 8-14; note that the boundary event was an instantaneous loss in diversity for the small articulate brachiopods but was only a final death blow to the already-declining ammonoid cephalopods.

Marked changes in terrestrial communities provide the most famous examples of Cretaceous diversity loss. The last of the dinosaurs, the dominant terrestrial vertebrates of the Mesozoic, died out at or very near the Cretaceous-Tertiary boundary. Dinosaurs, however, have a record of diversity decline more nearly comparable to that of cephalopods than brachiopods. By latest Cretaceous time, there were only a small number of dinosaurs—probably fewer than 20 species—stranded in habitats in the Western Interior region of North America. Thus, the termination of the dinosaurs represented a relatively small loss in species confined to a single region rather than a global massacre of diverse and abundant dinosaurs. (However, it can also be argued that there are relatively few places in the world where latest Cretaceous vertebrate faunas are well preserved; this low diversity of latest Cretaceous dinosaurs could thus be explained as due to taphonomic bias.)

FIG. 8-13 Overall diversity of ammonite cephalopod genera, expressed as taxa per million years; note that peak diversity occurs in mid-Cretaceous time and that the group declines throughout much of the Late Cretaceous (abbreviations indicate Cretaceous stage names). Percentage of "holdover taxa" reflects an increasing proportion of long-ranging ammonite genera held over from previous stages. (From P. D. Ward and P. W. Signor, 1983.)

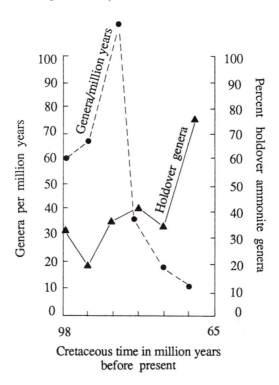

Cretaceous time in million years
before present

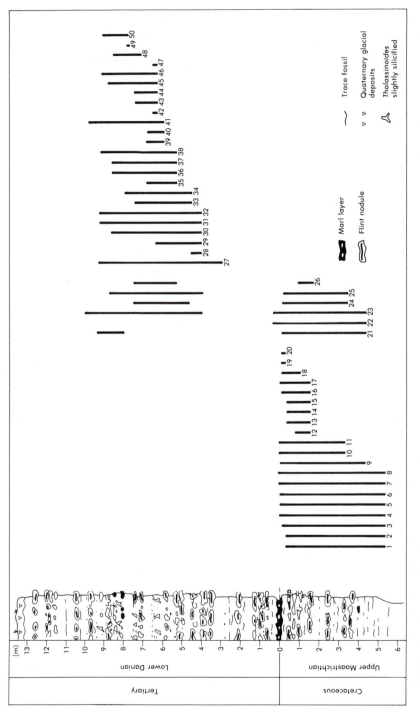

FIG. 8-14 Catastrophic disappearance of Cretaceous brachiopod species and subsequent stepwise appearance of Paleocene brachiopod species in the Cretaceous–Tertiary boundary interval at Nye Klov, Denmark. Numbers correspond to individual brachiopod species. (From F. Surlyk and M. B. Johansen, 1984, *Science*, v. 223, p. 1175. Copyright ©1984 by the AAAS.)

The paleoecology of the last dinosaurs and the timing of their final demise are still being argued. New discoveries of dinosaur remains in Arctic environments have raised the possibility that some dinosaurs may have been well equipped to withstand long periods of cold and darkness or instead were able to migrate long distances to regions south of the Arctic Circle, in order to avoid extreme cold and darkness. Another question that has been raised repeatedly is the issue of whether some dinosaurs may have survived the Cretaceous period only to go extinct in Early Tertiary time. Several workers have reported Tertiary occurrences of dinosaur bones, inferring a Tertiary rather than Cretaceous extinction for the group; however, other specialists have interpreted these occurrences as reworked Cretaceous bones in Tertiary strata (see Chapter 5 for discussion of reworking of vertebrate bones and teeth). In any case, almost all dinosaurs were extinct before the beginning of Tertiary time.

Cretaceous and Tertiary floras also record major environmental shifts associated with the mass extinction. Cretaceous climates were equable and very warm by present-day standards, and even in the midlatitudes the climates were largely aseasonal. The midlatitude flora of this time consisted predominantly of broad-leaved evergreen vegetation, with deciduous vegetation of only secondary importance; in the Northern Hemisphere deciduous trees were dominant only north of 66°N. In contrast, Paleocene climates in these latitudes were strongly seasonal, and in the midlatitudes floras were dominated by successional deciduous forests (Fig. 8-15). Jack Wolfe and colleagues at the U.S. Geological Survey have linked this evolutionary transition from evergreen to deciduous biotas with ecological disruption related to cooling during the Cretaceous mass extinction. This environmental disturbance led to heavy extinctions in evergreens relative to the deciduous plants. Thus, one answer to the question, "How did temperate deciduous forests arise?" is, "Through enhanced survival in the Cretaceous extinction." Mass extinctions may have been responsible for many such cases of evolutionary replacement in the fossil record.

Mechanisms for the Cretaceous extinction are controversial, but the widespread occurrence of the iridium anomaly as documented by W. Alvarez, L. Alvarez, and coworkers (see preceding material) indicates a meteorite impact at the Cretaceous-Tertiary boundary. This is the only one of the first-order extinctions to have been linked with global evidence for an impact. Unquestionably, many of the marine plankton extinctions correlate precisely with the level of the anomaly. More puzzling, however, are the numerous groups, such as ammonoid cephalopods and dinosaurs, that had already lost much taxonomic diversity in declines spanning millions of years, predating the end of the Cretaceous period. The impact model can well account for instantaneous disappearances, but how can it explain these gradual, attritional losses? Possibly the end of the Cretaceous was already an episode of global environmental stress, so that the environmental deterioration generated by the meteorite impact may have been only the final blow. Alternatively, perhaps there were several meteorite impacts rather than a single one, so that there were several widespread extinctions spread over latest Cretaceous time. Some researchers

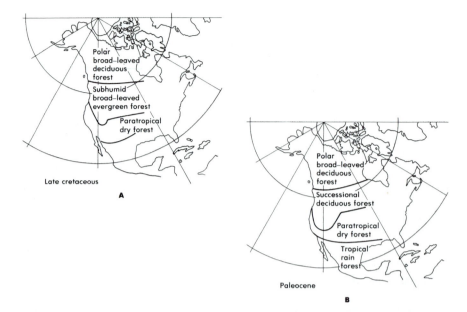

FIG. 8-15 Major floral patterns in the mid- to high latitudes of the Western Interior region of North America during Cretaceous (A) and Paleocene (B) time. Note that the Cretaceous evergreen community was replaced in the Paleocene time by a successional flora of deciduous forests. (Modified from J. A. Wolfe and G. R. Upchurch, 1986, *Nature,* v. 324, p. 148. Copyright © 1986 Macmillan Magazines Ltd.)

are arguing that such "stepped extinctions" may describe the Late Cretaceous mass extinction better than one single meteorite impact. Thus, though the impact theory of mass extinction does find considerable support in evidence from the Cretaceous event, some important extinction patterns still have not been adequately explained.

IMPLICATIONS OF MASS EXTINCTIONS

The contrast in extinction rate between steady-state or background extinction typical of most of the Phanerozoic fossil record and the intensified mass extinctions requires a quantitative difference between background and mass extinctions. However, there are also important qualitative differences in patterns of extinction during background versus mass extinction. For instance, David Jablonski, of the University of Chicago, has shown that during background intervals Cretaceous gastropods and bivalves with planktotrophic (plankton-feeding) larvae have longer species durations than those with nonplanktotrophic larvae (Fig. 8-16). In contrast, during the Cretaceous mass extinction, larval type apparently was not a factor in determining survivorship, for planktotrophic and nonplanktotrophic genera have identical frequencies of extinction. Jablonski has inferred from this that patterns and processes of extinction and survival may be fundamentally different in background intervals and mass extinction intervals.

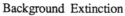

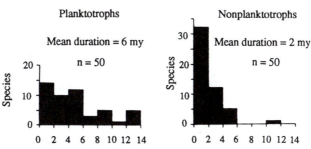

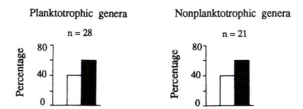

FIG. 8-16 Species durations for Late Cretaceous gastropods during background intervals (left) and during the Cretaceous mass extinctions (right). Note that during background time larval planktotrophy correlates with longer mean species durations; in contrast, during the Cretaceous mass extinction planktotrophs and nonplanktotrophs have comparable frequencies of survivor and victims. (From D. Jablonski, 1986.)

The contrasting pattern and processes in background versus mass extinction has several major implications for analysis of the history of life. First, if factors governing survivorship during "normal" intervals are not a reliable predictor of survival for mass extinctions, then other processes typical of globally stressed environments must be operative. Also, as extremely large fractions (50 to 95 percent) of the world's species are eliminated, the survival and extinction of some species may be due to chance or random effects rather than to predetermined factors. It is also important to recognize that each of the mass extinctions represents a paleoecological "filter" that controls the composition of all subsequent faunas and floras on Earth. Finally, mass extinctions, in eliminating much of the earth's biological diversity, also open ecological space, providing ecological opportunities for the evolutionary radiation of new forms.

SUMMARY

Throughout this book we have emphasized the inextricable link between organisms and environments, in which environmental conditions elicit biological responses, and biological activities, in turn, shape the physical and chemical environment. Mass extinctions result from environmental disturbances of such severity that normal biological responses are insufficient to ensure survival for many species. In these biological crises, both patterns and processes of extinction differ from those of normal or background intervals, and tremendous numbers of species are lost—up to 50 to 95 percent of all marine species in some of the largest extinctions. Five major mass extinctions stand out in the Phanerozoic diversity record; along with these are numerous minor extinction events, which vary in intensity and global significance. For the last 250 million years, extinctions may possibly have been rhythmic, occurring on average once every 26 million years.

The origin of mass extinctions has not been fully resolved, but several interesting hypotheses have been set forth. These possibilities include global cooling, global changes in sea level, and impact of asteroids or comets with the earth. Each of these ideas has scientific merits, but for each model there are also significant questions that need to be resolved. Indeed, more research may show that no single model can possibly account for all the extinctions; rather, the simple phrase "mass extinction" may summarize the result of many complex environmental factors. In this sense mass extinctions may be comparable to political revolutions, which represent times of accelerated social change but which may result from a variety of historical circumstances. Because there are so many exciting and unresolved questions, research on mass extinctions presents a continuing challenge for paleoecology and environmental stratigraphy.

SUGGESTIONS FOR FURTHER READING

CHAPTER 1

GEOLOGIC ENVIRONMENTS

AGER, D. V. 1963. *Principles of Paleoecology.* New York: McGraw-Hill.

GROSS, M. G. 1987. *Oceanography,* 4th ed. Englewood Cliffs, N.J.: Prentice-Hall.

IMBRIE, J., and N. D. NEWELL, eds. 1964. *Approaches to Paleoecology.* New York: Wiley.

LEVINTON, J. S. 1982. *Marine Ecology.* Englewood Cliffs, N.J.: Prentice-Hall.

MILLER, W. M., III. 1986. Paleoecology of benthic community replacement. *Lethaia* 19:225–31.

SIMPSON, G. G. 1963. "Historical Science." In *The Fabric of Geology,* edited by C. C. Albritton, Jr., 24–48. Reading, Mass.: Addison-Wesley.

CHAPTER 2

SEDIMENTS AND ENVIRONMENTS

ALLEN, J. R. L. 1970. *Physical Processes of Sedimentation.* New York: American Elsevier.

ALLEN, J. R. L. 1982. *Sedimentary Structures: Their Character and Physical Basis.* New York: Elsevier.

BATHURST, R. G. C. 1971. *Carbonate Sediments and Their Diagenesis.* New York: American Elsevier.

BLATT, H., G. MIDDLETON, and R. MURRAY. 1972. *Origin of Sedimentary Rocks.* Englewood Cliffs, N.J.: Prentice-Hall.

MATTHEWS, R. K. 1984. *Dynamic Stratigraphy,* 2nd ed. Englewood Cliffs, N.J.: Prentice-Hall.

SELLEY, R. C. 1976. *Introduction to Sedimentology.* New York: Academic Press.

REINECK, H., and I. B. SINGH. 1973. *Depositional Sedimentary Environments—with Reference to Terrigenous Clastics.* Berlin: Springer-Verlag.

CHAPTER 3

DEPOSITIONAL SYSTEMS AND ENVIRONMENTS

PAYTON, C., ed. 1977. *Seismic Stratigraphy—Applications to Hydrocarbon Exploration.* Tulsa: American Association of Petroleum Geologists, Mem. 26.

READING, H. G., ed. 1987. *Sedimentary Environments and Facies,* 2nd ed. Oxford: Blackwell.

SCHOLLE, P. A., and D. SPEARING, eds. *Sandstone Depositional Environments.* Tulsa: American Association of Petroleum Geologists.

SCHOLLE, P. A., D. G. BEBOUT, and C. H. MOORE. 1983. *Carbonate Depositional Environments.* Tulsa: American Association of Petroleum Geologists.

WALKER, R. G., ed. 1980. *Facies Models.* Toronto: Geological Association of Canada.

WILSON, J. L. 1975. *Carbonate Facies in Geologic History.* New York: Springer-Verlag.

CHAPTER 4

ORGANISMS AND ENVIRONMENTS

BARNES, R. S. K., and R. N. HUGHES. 1982. *An Introduction to Marine Ecology.* Oxford: Blackwell.

HEDGPETH, J. W., and H. LADD, eds. 1957. Treatise on marine ecology and paleoecology. *Geol. Soc. Am., Mem.* 67, 2 vols.

LEVINTON, J. S. 1982. *Marine Ecology.* Englewood Cliffs, N.J.: Prentice-Hall.

McCALL, P. L., and M. J. S. TEVESZ, eds. 1982. *Animal-Sediment Relations.* New York: Plenum.

ODUM, E. P. 1971. *Fundamentals of Ecology.* Philadelphia: Saunders.

RHOADS, D. C., and R. A. LUTZ. 1980. *Skeletal Growth of Aquatic Organisms.* New York: Plenum.

SCHÄFER, W. 1972. *Ecology and Palaeoecology of Marine Environments.* Chicago: University of Chicago Press.

SIMPSON, G. G., and W. BECK. 1965. *Life: An Introduction to Biology,* 2d ed. New York: Harcourt, Brace and World.

TEVESZ, M. J. S., and P. L. McCALL, eds. 1983. *Biotic Interactions in Recent and Fossil Benthic Communities.* New York: Plenum.

CHAPTER 5

TAPHONOMY

BEHRENSMEYER, A. K. 1975. The taphonomy and paleoecology of Plio-Pleistocene vertebrate assemblages east of Lake Rudolf, Kenya. *Mus. Comp. Zool. Bull.* 146:473–578.

BEHRENSMEYER, A. K., and A. P. HILL. 1980. *Fossils in the Making.* Chicago: University of Chicago Press.

BEHRENSMEYER, A. K., and S. M. KIDWELL. 1985. Taphonomy's contribution to paleobiology. *Paleobiology* 11:105–19.

CUMMINS, H., E. N. POWELL, R. J. STANTON, Jr., and G. STAFF. 1986. The rate of taphonomic loss in modern benthic habitats: how much of the potentially preservable community is preserved? *Palaeogeog., Palaeoclimatol., Palaeoecol.* 52:291–320.

BRETT, C. E., and G. C. BAIRD, eds. 1986. Taphonomy: ecology's loss is sedimentology's gain. *Palaios* 1(no. 3).

LAWRENCE, D. R. 1968. Taphonomy and information losses in fossil communities. *Geol. Soc. Am. Bull.* 79:1315–30.

MUELLER, A. H. 1979. "Fossilization (Taphonomy)." In *Treatise on Invertebrate Paleontology,* Pt. A, A1–A78. Geological Society of America and University of Kansas.

WARME, J. 1971. Paleoecological aspects of a modern coastal lagoon. *Univ. Calif. Publ. Geol. Sci.* 87:1–112.

CHAPTER 6

ENVIRONMENTAL ANALYSIS

BROECKER, W. S. 1974. *Chemical Oceanography.* New York: Harcourt Brace Jovanovich.

CURRAN, H. A., ed. 1985. *Biogenic Structures and Their Use in Interpreting Depositional Environments.* Soc. Econ. Paleontologists and Mineralogists, Spec. Publ. 35.

DODD, J. R., and R. J. STANTON. 1981. *Paleoecology: Concepts and Applications.* New York: Wiley.

EKDALE, A. A., R. G. BROMLEY, and S. G. PEMBERTON. 1984. *Ichnology: The Use of Trace Fossils in Sedimentology and Stratigraphy.* Tulsa: Soc. Econ. Paleontologists and Mineralogists.

FRIEDMAN, G., ed. 1969. *Depositional Environments in Carbonate Rocks,* Soc. Econ. Paleontologists and Mineralogists. Spec. Publ. 14.

HECKER, R. F. 1965. *Introduction to Paleoecology.* New York: American Elsevier.

RIGBY, J. K., and W. K. HAMBLIN, eds. 1972. *Recognition of Ancient Sedimentary Environments.* Soc. Econ. Paleontologists and Mineralogists, Spec. Publ. 16.

SCOTT, R. W., and R. R. WEST, eds. 1976. *Structure and Classification of Paleocommunities.* Stroudsburg, Pa.: Dowden, Hutchinson, and Ross.

SHAW, A. B. 1964. *Time in Stratigraphy.* New York: McGraw-Hill.

VALENTINE, J. W. 1973. *Evolutionary Paleoecology of the Marine Biosphere.* Englewood Cliffs, N.J.: Prentice-Hall.

CHAPTER 7

ENVIRONMENTAL SYNTHESIS

DODSON, P., A. K. BEHRENSMEYER, R. T. BAKKER, and J. S. McINTOSH. 1980. Taphonomy and paleoecology of the dinosaur beds of the Jurassic Morrison Formation. *Paleobiology* 6:209.

IMBRIE, J. 1985. A theoretical framework for the Pleistocene ice ages. *Jour. Geol. Soc. London* 142:423.

KENNETT, J. P., ed. 1985. *The Miocene Ocean.* Boulder, Colo.: Geol. Soc. Amer. Mem. 163.

KIPP, N. 1976. Investigation of late Quaternary paleoceanography and paleoclimatology. *Geol. Soc. Am., Mem.* 145:25.

LAPORTE, L. 1969. *Depositional environments in carbonate rocks.* Soc. Econ. Paleontologists and Mineralogists, Spec. Publ. 14:101.

PISCIOTTO, K. A., and R. E. GARRISON. 1981. "Lithofacies and depositional environments of the Monterey Formation, California." In *The Monterey Formation and Related Siliceous Rocks of California.* Soc. Econ. Paleontologists and Mineralogists, Pacific Section Guidebook, 103.

CHAPTER 8

ENVIRONMENTS IN CRISIS

ALVAREZ, L., W. ALVAREZ, F. ASARO, and H. V. MICHEL. 1980. Extraterrestrial cause for the Cretaceous-Tertiary extinction. *Science* 208:1095–1108.

ELLIOTT, D. K., ed. 1986. *Dynamics of Extinction.* New York: Wiley.

NEWELL, N. D. 1963. Crises in the history of life. *Sci. Am.* 208:76–92.

RAUP, D. M. 1986. *The Nemesis Affair.* New York: Norton.

SCHOPF, T. J. M. 1974. Permo-Triassic extinctions: relation to sea-floor spreading. *J. Geol.* 82:129–43.

SILVER, L. T., and P. H. SCHULTZ, eds. *Geological Implications of Impacts of Large Asteroids and Comets on the Earth.* Geological Society of America, Spec. Paper 190.

STANLEY, S. M. 1987. *Extinction.* New York: Scientific American.

STANLEY, S. M. 1988. Paleozoic mass extinctions: shared patterns suggest global cooling as a common cause. *Am. J. Sci.* 288:334–52.

CREDITS

CHAPTER 1

Figure   1-1   Courtesy of the Milwaukee Public Museum.

           1-2   Miller, W. 1986. Paleoecology of benthic community replacement. *Lethaia* 19:227.

           1-3   Pelletier, B. R. 1958. Pocono paleocurrents in Pennsylvania and Maryland. *Geol. Soc. Am. Bull.* 69:1055.

           1-5   Valentine, J. W. 1973. *Evolutionary Paleoecology of the Marine Biosphere.* Englewood Cliffs, N.J.: Prentice-Hall, 119.

           1-6   Aero Photographers.

Table   1-1   Crosby, E. J. 1972. *Recognition of Ancient Sedimentary Environments.* Soc. Econ. Paleontologists and Mineralogists, Spec. Publ. 16, 10.

CHAPTER 2

Figure   2-1   Laporte, L. F. 1975. *Encounter with the Earth.* San Francisco: Canfield Press, 163.

           2-2   Press, F., and R. Siever. 1974. *Earth.* San Francisco: W. H. Freeman and Company, 291.

           2-3   Weller, J. M. 1960. *Stratigraphic Principles and Practice.* New York: Harper and Row, 341.

           2-4   A,E—Courtesy of Henry Mullins, Syracuse University.

           2-4   B,C,D—Pettijohn, F. J., and P. Potter. 1964. *Atlas and Glossary of Primary Structures.* New York: Springer-Verlag.

           2-5   Ingle, J. C., Jr. 1975. *Current Concepts of Depositional Systems with Applications for Petroleum Geology.* San Joaquin Geol. Soc., 2–4.

           2-6   Allen, J. R. L. 1970. *Physical Processes of Sedimentation.* New York: American Elsevier, 205.

           2-7   Folk, R. L., and R. Robles. 1964. Carbonate sands of Isla Perez, Alacran reef complex, Yucatan. *J. Geol.* 72:267.

           2-8   Courtesy of D. C. Rhoads, Yale University.

           2-9   Ginsburg, R. N. 1957. *Regional Aspects of Carbonate Deposition.* Soc. Econ. Paleontologists and Mineralogists, Spec. Publ. 5, 82.

        2-10   A, B, C—Logan, B. W., R. Rezak, and R. N. Ginsburg. 1964, Classification and environmental significance of stromatolites. *J. Geol.* 72:72, Plate 1A, 3C.
D—Rezak, R. 1957. *Stromatolites of the Belt Series in Glacier National Park and Vicinity, Montana.* U.S. Geol. Surv. Prof. Paper 294-D, Plate 21-8.
E—Hofmann, H. 1969. *Attributes of Stromatolites.* Geol. Surv. Canada, Paper 69-39, 4.

        2-11   A and B—Ginsburg, R. N., and H. A. Lowenstam. 1958. The influence of marine bottom communities on the depositional environment of sediments. *J. Geol.* 66:31.
C—Matthews, R. K. 1974. *Dynamic Stratigraphy.* Englewood Cliffs, N.J.: Prentice-Hall, 230.

Table   2-1   See Fig. 2-1, p. 47.

           2-2   McAlester, A. L. 1977. *The History of Life.* Englewood Cliffs, N.J.: Prentice-Hall, 53.

CHAPTER 3

Figure   3-1   Kauffman, E. G. 1984. "Paleobiogeography and evolutionary response dynamic in the Cretaceous Western Interior Seaway of North America." In *Jurassic-*

Cretaceous Biochronology and Paleogeography of North America, edited by G. E. G. Westermann, 276. Toronto: University of Toronto Press.

3-2 Vail, P. R., R. M. Mitchum, and S. Thompson. 1977. Seismic stratigraphy and global changes in sealevel. Pt. 4: Global cycles of relative changes in sealevel. In *Seismic Stratigraphy—Applications to Hydrocarbon Exploration,* edited by C. E. Payton, 84. Tulsa: American Association of Petroleum Geologists.

3-4 Graham, S. A. 1975. *Current Concepts of Depositional Systems with Applications to Petroleum Geology.* San Joaquin Geol. Soc., 0–3.

3-6 See Fig. 3-4, p. 0–5.

3-8 See Fig. 3-4, p. 0–4.

3-10 See Fig. 3-4, p. 0–4.

3-11 See Fig. 3-4, p. 0–7.

3-12 Walker, R. G. 1979. "Turbidites and associated coarse clastic deposits." In *Facies Models,* edited by R. G. Walker, 98. Toronto: Geological Association of Canada.

3-13 See Fig. 3-12, p. 99.

3-14 Kennett, J. 1982. *Marine Geology.* Englewood Cliffs, N.J.: Prentice-Hall, 465.

3-15 A—Davies, T. A., and D. S. Gorsline. 1976. "Oceanic sediments and sedimentary processes." In *Chemical Oceanography,* edited by J. P. Riley and R. Chester, 71. New York: Academic Press.
B—Garrison, R. E. 1974. "Radiolarian cherts, pelagic limestones and igneous rocks in engeosyclinal assemblages." In *Pelagic Sediments: On Land and under the Sea,* edited by K. J. Hsü and H. C. Jenkyns. Oxford: Blackwell.

3-16 Hersey, J. B. 1963. *Continuous reflection profiling.* Vol. 3 of *The Sea,* edited by M. N. Hill, 47. (editor), New York: Wiley.

3-17 Courtesy of Henry Mullins, Syracuse University.

3-18 Courtesy of Henry Mullins, Syracuse University.

CHAPTER 4

Figure 4-2 Jablonski, D. 1986. Larval ecology and macroevolution in marine invertebrates. *Bull. Marine Sci.* 39:573.

4-3 Newell, N. D., and D. W. Boyd. 1985. Permian scallops of the pectinacean family Streblochondriidae. *Am. Mus. Nov.* no. 2831:7.

4-4 McMahon, R. F., and W. D. Russell-Hunter. 1977. Temperature relations of aerial and aquatic respiration in six littoral snails in relation to their vertical zonation. *Biol. Bull.* 152:186.

4-5 Parsons, T. R., M. Takahashi, and B. Hargrave. 1979. *Biological Oceanographic Processes,* 2d ed. New York: Pergamon, 80.

4-6 Thompson, J. B., H. T. Mullins, C. R. Newton, and T. L. Vercoutere. 1985. Alternative biofacies model for dysaerobic communities. *Lethaia* 18:168.

4-7 See Fig. 4-6, p. 170.

4-8 Segerstråle, S. A. 1957. Treatise on Marine Ecology. *Geol. Soc. Am., Mem.* 1(67):777.

4-9 Valentine, J. W. 1973. *Evolutionary Paleoecology of the Marine Biosphere.* Englewood Cliffs, N.J.: Prentice-Hall, 166.

4-10 A,C—Ekdale, A. A., R. G. Bromley, and S. G. Pemberton. 1984. *Ichnology: Trace Fossils in Sedimentology and Stratigraphy.* Tulsa: Soc. Econ. Paleontologists and Mineralogists, 14, 70.
B—Frey, R. W. 1975. *Trace Fossils.* New York: Springer-Verlag, 25.

4-11 Purdy, E. G. 1964. "Sediments as Substrates." In *Approaches to Paleoecology,* edited by J. Imbrie and N. D. Newell, 260. New York: Wiley.
Newell, N. D., J. Imbrie, E. G. Purdy, and D. L. Thurber. 1959. Organism communities and bottom facies, Great Bahama Bank. *Am. Mus. Nat. Hist. Bull.* 117:202.
Enos, P. 1974. *Surface sediment facies of the Florida-Bahamas Plateau.* Geol. Soc. Am. Map.

4-12 Odum, E. P. 1971. *Fundamentals of Ecology.* Philadelphia: Saunders, 191.

4-13 Russell-Hunter, W. D. 1970. *Aquatic Productivity.* New York: Macmillan, 43.

4-14   Cushing, D. H. 1975. *Marine Ecology and Fisheries.* London: Cambridge University Press, p. 17.

4-15   Data from Ryther, J. 1969. Photosynthesis and fish production in the sea. *Science* 166: 72–76.

4-16   Zaret, T. M., and R. T. Paine. 1973. Species introduction in a tropical lake. *Science* 182:452.

4-17   Hessler, R. R., and W. M. Smithey, Jr. 1983. "The community structure of megafauna." In *Hydrothermal Processes at Seafloor Spreading Centers,* edited by P. A. Rona, K. Boström, L. Laubier, and K. L. Smith, Jr., 764. New York: Plenum.

Table   4-1   Butler, P. 1953. Oyster growth as affected by latitudinal temperature gradients. *Comm. Fish. Rev.* 352:7–12.

CHAPTER 5

Figure   5-1   Behrensmeyer, A. K., and S. M. Kidwell. 1985. Taphonomy's contributions to paleobiology. *Paleobiology* 11:108.

5-2   Behrensmeyer, A. K. 1975. The taphonomy and paleoecology of Plio-Pleistocene vertebrate assemblages east of Lake Rudolf, Kenya. *Mus. Comp. Zool. Bull.* 146:493.

5-3   Brain, C. K. 1980. "Some criteria for the recognition of bone-collecting agencies in African caves." In *Fossils in the Making,* edited by A. K. Behrensmeyer and A. P. Hill, 114. Chicago: University of Chicago Press.

5-4   See Fig. 4-10 A, p. 90.

5-5   Signor, P. 1985. "Real and apparent trends in species richness through time." In *Phanerozoic Diversity Patterns,* edited by J. W. Valentine, 130, 136. Princeton, N.J.: Princeton University Press.

5-6   Conway Morris, S. H. B. Whittington, D. E. B. Briggs, C. P. Hughes, and D. L. Bruton. 1982. *Atlas of the Burgess Shale.* Palaeontological Association, Figs. F,I,W.

Table   5-1   Voorhies, M. R. 1969. *Taphonomy and Population Dynamics of an Early Pliocene Vertebrate Fauna, Knox Co., Nebraska.* Contrib. to Geology, Univ. Wyoming, Spec. Paper 1, 69.

5-2   Warme, J. 1971. Paleoecological aspects of a modern coastal lagoon. *Univ. Calif. Publ. Geol. Sci.* 87:94.

5-3   Schindel, D. E. 1980. Microstratigraphic sampling and the limits of paleontologic resolution. *Paleobiology* 6:408–26.

5-4   Lawrence, D. R. 1968. Taphonomy and information losses in fossil communities. *Geol. Soc. Am. Bull.* 79:1323.

5-5   See Table 5-4, p. 1325.

5-6   See Table 5-4, p. 1326.

CHAPTER 6

Figure   6-2   See Fig. 4-10 A,C, p. 24.

6-3   See Fig. 4-10 A,C, p. 187.

6-4   Duplessy, J. C. 1978. "Isotopic Studies." In *Climatic Change,* edited by J. Gribben, 633. London: Cambridge University Press.

6-5   Jones, D. S., D. F. Williams, and C. S. Romanek. 1986. Life history of symbiont-bearing giant clams from stable isotope profiles. *Science* 231:46.

6-6   Vergnaud-Grazzini, C. 1985. "Mediterranean late Cenozoic stable isotope record: stratigraphic and paleoclimatic implications." In *Geological Evolution of the Mediterranean Basin,* edited by D. J. Stanley, and F. C. Wezel, 420, 423. New York: Springer-Verlag.

6-7   Garrels, R. M., and Mackenzie, F. T. 1971. *Evolution of Sedimentary Rocks.* New York: W. W. Norton and Co., Inc., p. 91.
Arthur, M. A., T. F. Anderson, I. R. Kaplan, J. Veizer, and L. S. Land. Stable isotopes in sedimentary geology. *Soc. Econ. Paleontologists and Mineralogists Short Course Notes,* 10:1–84.

6-8 Scholle, P. A., and M. A. Arthur. 1980. Carbon isotope fluctuations in Cretaceous pelagic limestone. *Amer. Assoc. Petrol. Geol. Bull.* 64:72.

6-9 Sanders, H. 1968. Marine benthic diversity: a comparative study. *Amer. Naturalist* 102:250.

6-10 Scott, R. W. 1978. Approaches to trophic analysis of paleocommunities. *Lethaia* 11:11.

CHAPTER 7

Figure 7-1 Laporte, L. 1969. *Depositional environments in carbonate rocks.* Soc. Econ. Paleontologists and Mineralogists, Spec. Publ. 14, 101.

7-2 See Fig. 7-1, p. 103.

7-3 See Fig. 7-1, p. 104.

7-4 See Fig. 7-1, p. 116.

7-5 Dodson, P., A. K. Behrensmeyer, R. T. Bakker, and J. S. McIntosh. 1980. Taphonomy and paleoecology of the dinosaur beds of the Jurassic Morrison Formation. *Paleobiology* 6:209.

7-6 Bakker, R. 1986. *The Dinosaur Heresies.* New York: Morrow, 106.

7-7 Stanley, S. 1986. *Earth and Life Through Time.* New York: W. H. Freeman and Company, 460.

7-8 See Fig. 7-5, p. 224.

7-9 See Fig. 7-5, p. 225.

7-10 See Fig. 7-6, p. 192.

7-11 Pisciotto, K. A., and R. E. Garrison. 1981. "Lithofacies and depositional environments of the Monterey Formation, California." In *The Monterey Formation and Related Siliceous Rocks of California.* Soc. Econ. Paleontologists and Mineralogists, Pacific Section Guidebook, 103.

7-12 A, B—Courtesy of Marcia Gowing, University of California, Santa Cruz. C—Garrison, R. E. 1981. "Pelagic and hemipelagic sedimentation in active margin basins." In *Depositional Systems of Active Continental Margin Basins.* Soc. Econ. Paleontologists and Mineralogists, Pacific Section Short Course Notes, 20, 24.

7-13 Barrera, E., G. Keller, and S. M. Savin. 1985. Evolution of the Miocene ocean in the eastern North Pacific as inferred from oxygen and carbon isotopic ratios of foraminifera. *Geol. Soc. Am., Mem.* 163:89.

7-14 Ericson, D., and G. Wollin. 1961. Atlantic deep-sea cores. *Geol. Soc. America Bull.* 72:265; 1964, *The Deep and the Past.* New York: Knopf.

7-15 Ericson, D., and G. Wollin. 1964. *The Deep and the Past.* New York: Knopf, 89.

7-16 Ericson, D., and G. Wollin. 1961. Atlantic deep-sea cores. *Geol. Soc. Am. Bull.* 72:277.

7-17 A—Kipp, N. 1976. Investigation of late Quaternary paleoceanography and paleoclimatology, *Geol. Soc. Am., Mem.* 145:25. B—McIntyre, A., and others. Investigation of late Quaternary paleoceanography and paleoclimatology. *Geol. Soc. Am., Mem.* 145:51.

7-18 Imbrie, J., and N. Kipp. 1971. *The Late Cenozoic Glacial Ages.* New Haven: Yale University Press, 118.

7-19 See Fig. 7-17(B), 59.

7-20 B—Imbrie, J. 1985. A theoretical framework for the Pleistocene ice ages. *Jour. Geol. Soc. London.* 142:423.

7-21 See Fig. 7-20(B), 426.

Table 7-1 See Fig. 7-1, 105.

CHAPTER 8

Figure 8-1 Raup, D. M., and J. J. Sepkoski. 1982. Mass extinctions in the marine fossil record. *Science* 215:1501.

8-2 See Fig. 8-1, p. 1502.

8-3 Raup, D. M., and J. J. Sepkoski. 1986. Periodic extinction of families and genera. *Science* 231:834.

8-4   Teichert, C. 1986. Times of crisis in the evolution of the Cephalopoda: *Palaeont. Zeit.* 60:238.

8-5   Schopf, T. J. M. 1974. Permo-Triassic extinctions: relation to sea-floor spreading. *J. Geol.* 82:131.

8-6   Alvarez, L. W., W. Alvarez, F. Asaro, and H. V. Michel. 1980. Extraterrestrial cause for the Cretaceous-Tertiary extinction. *Science* 208:1099.

8-7   Alvarez, W., L. Alvarez, F. Asaro, and H. V. Michel. 1982. "Current status of the impact theory for the terminal Cretaceous extinction." In *Geological Implications of Impacts of Large Asteroids and Comets on the Earth,* edited by L. T. Silver and P. H. Schultz. Geological Society of America Spec. Paper 190, 306.

8-8   Courtesy of B. F. Bohor, U.S. Geological Survey.

8-9   Courtesy of NASA.

8-10   Stanley, S. M. 1986. *Earth and Life through Time.* New York: W. H. Freeman and Company, 411.

8-11   Padian, K., and W. A. Clemens. 1985. "Terrestrial vertebrate diversity: episodes and insights." In *Phanerozoic Diversity Patterns,* edited by J. W. Valentine, 57. Princeton, N.J.: Princeton University Press.

8-12   Niklas, K. J., B. H. Tiffney, and A. H. Knoll. 1985. "Patterns in vascular land plant diversification: an analysis at the species level." In *Phanerozoic Diversity Patterns,* edited by J. W. Valentine, 107. Princeton, N.J.: Princeton University Press.

8-13   Ward, P. D., and P. W. Signor. 1983. Evolutionary tempo in Jurassic and Cretaceous ammonites. *Paleobiology* 9:196.

8-14   Surlyk, F., and M. B. Johansen. 1984. End-Cretaceous brachiopod extinctions in the chalk of Denmark. *Science* 223:1175.

8-15   Wolfe, J. A., and G. R. Upchurch. 1986. Vegetation, climatic and floral changes at the Cretaceous-Tertiary boundary. *Nature* 324:148.

8-16   Jablonski, D. 1986. Background and mass extinctions: the alternation of macroevolutionary regimes. *Science* 231:130.

INDEX

Peritidal environment, 9
Permian period, mass extinctions in, 141,
　143, 145, 146, 151–52, 154
Phanerozoic period, 39, 40, 93, 158
　fossil record, 12
　mass extinctions in, 140–41, 145, 151,
　　152
Phosphorus, 63
Photic zone, 8
Photoinhibition, 63, 64
Photoplankton, 63, 64, 74, 75, 77
Pleistocene period:
　glaciation, 1–2, 11–12, 18, 33, 53, 54,
　　102, 137
　Koobi Formation, 123
　North Atlantic Ocean during, 113,
　　127–37
Poaline silica, 91
Pocono Formation, 6
Point bar deposits, 40
Point Sur, California, 65, 66
Precambrian rocks, 30

Q

Quartz grains, 148
Quaternary period, 135, 146

R

Raup, David, 12, 140–43, 148
Reduced floodplain mudstones, 119
Reef facies, 39, 47, 48
"Refrigeration" theory, 146
Ripple marks, 22–24
Rondout Formation, 114

S

Salinity:
　of Caribbean Sea, 133, 134
　isotopic composition, 104,
　organisms and, 65–67

Salt marsh, 44–45
Sea level, lowering of, 144–45, 152
Sedimentary rocks:
　origin and classification of major, 17
　texture, 20
Sediments, 15–35
　biogenic structures and, 28–33
　burrowing of marine invertebrates and,
　　34
　clastic, 16, 38
　cores, 128–34
　cross-stratification, 22, 23
　currents and, 18–20
　deposition of, 36–56
　graded bedding, 25
　grain size, 20–21, 68
　ice and, 18
　mud cracks and, 23, 24
　nonclastic, 16
　organic influences on, 26–34
　origins of, 15–17
　primary structures of, 21–26
　rates of weathering, effect on, 16–17
　reconstruction of ancient environments,
　　97–99
　ripple marks and, 22–24
　skeletal materials in, 26–28
　sole marks and, 24
　solution and, 17
　suspension and, 18
　traction and, 18
　transportation and deposition of, 17–21
　turbidite beds, 23, 25
　water velocity and, 20–21
　wind and, 18
Seismic-reflection profiling, 52–54
Seismic stratigraphy, 52–54
Selective deposit feeders, 71
Seneca Lake, 54
Sepkoski, Jack, 12, 140–43, 148
Serengeti Plain, 122, 123
Skeletal materials, 26–28
Sodium chloride, 66
Sole marks, 24
Solution, sediments and, 17
Stanley, Steven, 146
Straits of Gibraltar, 104
Stratigraphic sequence, 37–40

NOTES